From Dawn to Dusk:
A Hard Row to Hoe

From Dawn to Dusk: A Hard Row to Hoe

One Man's Story of Surviving the Great Depression, Dust Bowl and More.

Emery Carl Hinkhouse, Jr.

FROM DAWN TO DUSK: A HARD ROW TO HOE
ONE MAN'S STORY OF SURVIVING THE GREAT DEPRESSION, DUST BOWL AND MORE.

Copyright © 2018 Emery Carl Hinkhouse, Jr..

All rights reserved. No part of this book may be used or reproduced by any means, graphic, electronic, or mechanical, including photocopying, recording, taping or by any information storage retrieval system without the written permission of the author except in the case of brief quotations embodied in critical articles and reviews.

iUniverse books may be ordered through booksellers or by contacting:

iUniverse
1663 Liberty Drive
Bloomington, IN 47403
www.iuniverse.com
1-800-Authors (1-800-288-4677)

Because of the dynamic nature of the Internet, any web addresses or links contained in this book may have changed since publication and may no longer be valid. The views expressed in this work are solely those of the author and do not necessarily reflect the views of the publisher, and the publisher hereby disclaims any responsibility for them.

Any people depicted in stock imagery provided by Getty Images are models, and such images are being used for illustrative purposes only.
Certain stock imagery © Getty Images.

ISBN: 978-1-5320-6267-4 (sc)
ISBN: 978-1-5320-6269-8 (hc)
ISBN: 978-1-5320-6268-1 (e)

Library of Congress Control Number: 2018913515

Print information available on the last page.

iUniverse rev. date: 11/19/2018

Dedication

THIS BOOK IS dedicated to the one true love of my life, Evelyn, to whom I was happily married for seventy-two years and two months and two days. I will not be marrying again. No one could ever match her.

Evelyn Elvera "Nelson" and Emery Carl Hinkhouse Jr.

Thanks go to my children who helped
me with editing this book:
Joyce Lillich
Audrey Haskins
David Hinkhouse
Stephen Hinkhouse

T in the Road

Dedicated to my father, Emery C. Hinkhouse

In places west of thought the avenues have no names:
a boulder by the bend of a backwoods brook, a broken
branch pointing north over a backroad bridge and the ridge,
past Rebel Road, where memory lies discarded in the dust
of a weed-filled ditch of roosters chasing grasshoppers
from dawn to dusk while hound dogs loll in the shade
of giant black oak trees waiting for the next coon hunt.
We come to a T in the road that turns east back to town
or west deeper into the country of narrow gravel roads
and misfits who fell off the edge of the earth
and landed here where no one will remind them
of all the different ways they will never fit in.
Rusty trailers, tractors, and tin roofed huts dot yards
hidden by long driveways that lead off into dark woods
where, somehow, barefooted children find a way to survive
the loneliness they do not yet know how to describe.
Up and down hills 'til we finally reach the one-room school,
abandoned now, where you told us you walked seven miles
every day to attend, meeting your raggedy companions
along the way, down shortcut trails and loose gravel paths
to the final destination at the end of that turn we took to the west--
all the misfits in one room, alone no more, six rows of desks,
five desks per row, all full of the hope needed to face the future.

By my son, David A. Hinkhouse

Chapter 1

Hobson's Choice

I WAS BORN on December 18, 1917, in Correctionville, Iowa, near Sioux City. I lived there with my first father, who was my genetic father, for the first four years of my life. Then my mom and my dad, Emery (after whom I am named), got divorced and my new life began. All I knew was that they had trouble getting along and Dad decided to leave town. His leaving left a fire in my stomach that lingered for a long time. The memory of being shoved back and forth between them at the courthouse as they argued over who "had to take me" has stuck with me all my life. I was born with a "lazy eye" but I had no trouble seeing what was going on that day. Outside the courthouse, for some reason, I remember two crows hackling at each other overhead in the giant black oak trees, the heat, and I remember looking down at my shoes and shuffling my feet, feeling scared and alone. I didn't know that was the last time I would be wearing shoes in the summertime for a long time to come.

I guess the rest of my story starts there, since I don't have much memory of what happened before that, except for the arguments they had. I also remember feeling sorry for my mom even though it appeared she didn't want me to go with her. I ended up living with my mother and Goldie, my mentally handicapped, epileptic sister.

Mom remarried a hired hand named Allen Robinson, and we soon drove his car, a 1921 Model T touring car, to Missouri. We went via Highway 71, which at that time was only gravel in the worst spots. There were no fancy paved highways back then, just muddy roads and a little gravel. It was December 1922, and we traveled with no side curtains and no heater. I remember lying behind the front seat and covering up with an old wool army blanket. I wasn't happy with my new dad but never told anyone. I still wanted my real dad back at that point. My mom, stepdad, and sister all rode in the front seat, which was small in those old cars. The Model T rode pretty rough, especially over those rutted dirt roads. Needless to say, it was a joyless ride.

We got to Carroll, Iowa, late that first night and stayed in a hotel. There were no motels back then. The next day, we stopped about twelve miles south of our destination of Nevada, Missouri, and boy what a landing! We had come to a creek with no bridge, but my new dad's brothers, sisters, mom, dad, and the rest of our new in-laws met us. So, we had plenty of help pushing the car across the creek and up the hill.

When we got there, all we found was a log house with one big room and a kitchen downstairs and an attic room called the garret. It sure wasn't much to look at, but it was a roof over our heads after a long, hard trip that must have been very traumatic for my mom. It was my step-great-grandmother Bell's house. She had been widowed by her husband, who had accidentally killed himself demonstrating how to load his wartime musket, the gun he had used in the Civil War as a Confederate soldier. My new grandmother and grandfather, five single uncles, one single aunt, one uncle with his wife and two kids, and my mom and dad and Goldie and me were all to stay under one roof. I wondered where everyone would sleep.

When night came, all the men went to the attic and slept on the floor on straw mattresses. I slept with Charlie, my new cousin, who was about sixteen years old at the time. I formed a bond early on with Charlie, and it lasted a lifetime. I guess you could say he took me under his wing and made me feel included in the new family I was about to adopt.

My mom had gone from a land of plenty to a land of nothing overnight. Her life in Iowa had been in a family of "rich" farmers. No one had ever gone without food or clothes. At the first meal in our new log house, the kids had to stand beside their moms. I was not used to this, and I cried. My mom took me outside and spanked me real good. I soon learned to change my ways.

A lot happened that first winter. I remember watching them butcher their hog so we could eat. We hung it outside in a tree to bleed out. I learned really fast with five step-uncles to show me the ropes in my new life. That year went by pretty fast. I had my fifth birthday during that first winter in Missouri.

The next spring, in 1923, we moved again, beginning our second journey in the nomadic life of the poor and down-and-out. It was about then that I realized my life would become one big Hobson's choice. The horse I was about to ride was the only horse my mom and new step-dad offered and pretty much summed up my new life with the Robinson family. I had no choice but to make the best of it—get on and ride the broken-down swaybacked horse—if I wanted to survive.

Chapter 2

Hudson, Fenton, Nevins, Flynn Places

OUR THIRD "NEW" house was called the Elmer Hudson Place. It was located in Cedar County, six or seven miles northeast of Stockton, Missouri. My stepdad worked at the coal mines nearby. (From this point on, I will call him my dad because he's the only dad I ever had.) We were close to a creek on the edge of Ozark timberland filled with hickories, black oaks and walnut trees. It was all new to me.

In the fall of 1923, I went to my first school, Shady Hill School, located next to an old country store called Virgil. It was a one-room schoolhouse, and it was overcrowded, with two or three kids sharing each desk seat. Yes, we shared seats and thought nothing of it; there were no other options. (Author's aside: I laugh today when I hear of parents and teachers complaining about too many kids in the classroom. I guess we were the involuntary test cases so they could aim things in a better direction for future students and teachers.) But we all liked the closeness.

When I walked to school, I had to cross Turkey Creek, which had no bridge across the road. After another mile and a half, I had to cut through the timber, which lasted for another mile. My dad cut down a big tree so it would fall across the creek and provide a foot log for me. It was pretty scary the first time or two, but I soon got used to it. My sister, Goldie, didn't go to school that fall because she couldn't walk on the foot log. It was becoming clear to me at that point that she had problems learning. I would later realize that she had epilepsy, along with her difficulties with learning.

That fall there were a lot of snakes on our property. I hadn't learned which ones were poisonous, so I just killed every snake I saw. We had trouble with blacksnakes and possums eating our chickens' eggs. It was an ongoing battle we fought along with the other elements of Mother Nature that had us in a chokehold. We only stayed at that Elmer Hudson Place for a few months. My dad walked back to where we had spent our first winter with his parents, and he borrowed forty dollars from my great-grandmother, Bell. She got a forty-dollar monthly pension check for Great-Grandpa Bell's Civil War service. This was the life-saving money our family would use during very tough times in the 1920s. Many people don't realize that for poor farmers the Great Depression started in the 20's. It didn't catch up to city folks until the fall of 1929. We didn't have a name for it in the 1920s. We just knew that we went to bed hungry many nights. I don't think Dad ever paid Grandma Bell back. There was nothing to pay her back with during those times.

He bought two horses, a harness, and a wagon and came back to move us to our fourth farm since Mom's new marriage, the Fenton Place, about twelve miles south of Nevada, Missouri. Dad got home way after dark. I didn't know what a sharecropper was back then, but that's what we were.

I suspect we moved a lot so Dad and Mom could "better themselves" and find a bigger house, more farmland, and overall, better living conditions. That was hardly ever the case, though. This rental agreement was like all the others we had made as tenant farmers. It had two parts: (1) the typical grain crop split in which the tenant farmer got two-thirds and the owner one-third, and (2) a fixed rent of around fifty dollars per year. We really never cared much about the terms because both the landlord and we knew that if crops failed we would not be able to pay anything. That was pretty much the silent agreement between owner and sharecropper, which in a year of crop failures usually meant a move to the next farm for us. There would be many of those to come.

The next morning, we loaded what we could and started our forty-mile trip. We stopped at noon and ate what Mom had made and packed the night before. We also fed and watered the horses, who I had named Bess and Molly. They were three-year-old Mustangs from Montana. Dad had bought them from Mr. Gill Palmer, who we thought was a rich man because he owned oil wells in Oklahoma. Each year he would buy a railroad car full of wild mustangs that had been rounded up off the free range in Montana. He must have been quite a businessman with a lot of connections.

I always loved my horses and became a pretty good horseman over the years. Bess and Molly were a team and pulled plows and wagons, but we could also ride them. They were Western Mustangs. Molly was a bay mare and Bess was a mouse-colored mare. They were both very gentle and very easy to get along with. Pat, our other horse, was the one I rode most. He was a bay colored Montana Mustang.

It was at the Fenton place that I first learned the boxing skills that would serve me later in life. Palmer's son, Bill, was the first person to teach me a little about boxing. He showed me how to put up my fists and look through my gloves while facing an opponent. He told me to look for his face and, any time I saw an opening, to jab him. I always remembered this lesson, especially when I later fought in the CC Camps. That story will come later. Those skills served me well as life moved along.

We arrived at the Fenton Place sometime after dark and set up the stove so Mom could get supper ready. Then we prepared our beds. I waited for Mom to cook so I could start exploring the new place. The Fenton Place was like a mansion compared to the place we had farmed the year before. We now had a barn, a chicken house, a smokehouse, and a four-room house with a creek running behind it. My new job was to gather the kindling for starting fires in the stove for cooking and heat. I found every variety of trees up and down the creek, hickories, black oaks, cedar and maple.

Dad bought a cow for milk, and I learned to milk that very day. We owned that cow, Boss, for a long time, maybe five or six years. She was a Red Poll-Jersey mix, and she delivered a new calf for us each year. We generally sold it for veal, as we always needed the money now to put food on the table instead of later. Eventually, Dad decided to trade Boss for a full-bred Jersey because Boss was a "rogue" cow. She always tried to escape, rode fences down to do it, and Dad finally got tired of having to retrieve her.

Our school was called Sandstone, and it was about one and a half miles straight through the timber or two and a half miles around if I took the road. I generally went through the timber. It was a more interesting walk and faster. I saw lots of wildlife: deer, rabbits, snakes, raccoons, and the occasional skunk, among many others. At least this time we didn't have to cross a creek to get there, so my sister could now attend. The school had about forty-six students in grades one through eight, all in the same one-room schoolhouse, which sat on one acre of ground. One teacher, Miss Neva, taught everyone.

She was an old maid and very strict. The troublemakers would get a whipping, as we called it back then, if they were caught fighting. One day, I had one of my first real playground fights with a bully called Yader. A classmate, a tongue-tied boy named Thomas, told on us and said to Miss Neva, "Junior kicked Yader, and Yader kicked Junior ..." Everyone called me Junior because it was at the end of my name. We got in trouble that day. Back then the teacher had a paddle or a switch for discipline and was not shy about using those tools of tears.

My grandparents had moved back to the Sandstone school district, so Charlie—the one who had taken me under his wing when I was younger—and my other cousins Claude and Mary now went to my school. They all lived in a place that later became the Sandstone Store, which replaced the old store and was run by my stepuncle John Wells, Aunt Leddie's husband. Leddie was my stepdad's sister. This store will be featured in later memories.

I earned my first money living on the Fenton Place by cleaning out an attic for a blind lady, Mrs. Berry, who lived with her son, Jess Mills. I never asked why they had different last names. She paid me fifteen cents for a job that took all day to accomplish, in an attic during the hot Missouri summer. It was a pretty good day's pay.

On May 22, 1925, while we were still living at the Fenton Place, my new brother, Virgil, was born. He came in the midmorning, and Dr. Keithly traveled from Milo, Missouri, about five miles away, to assist with the birth. He charged twenty dollars. Milo was a "one-horse" town, with a general store run and owned by Mr. Glen Darling; a blacksmith shop; a grain elevator; and a bank run by a man named Ben Heart. Later, Mr. Heart would loan me ten dollars out of his own pocket at a crucial time in my life. More on that later.

In March 1927, we moved to our fifth tenant farm, the Nevins Place, two miles east of our Fenton Place and near the Round Prairie school. We always seemed to move in the spring, when it was cold and rainy. We lived near the Pilchers—a large extended family that lived across the countryside. They were kind of like the Hatfields or McCoys, clanlike, with the types of behaviors you would expect from those sorts of families. Their houses had dirt floors, and pigs could be seen running in and out of the houses at just about any time of day. Much later, after I married my wife, Evelyn, Elmo Pilcher, then about sixty years old, died of cancer, Evelyn prayed over him in his final days. I have told many stories about the Pilchers through the years, and I guess I used them as a sort of standard for the type of life I would be heading away from.

I liked moving, but I didn't like changing schools. After the first day, it was okay, though. I now had only a mile-and-a-half walk to school on a main road, which was pretty close considering the other places we had lived. For the first time, I had a male teacher. His name was Herbert Cooper and he was only eighteen years old. He was teaching in his first year out of high school. Teachers didn't have to have a college degree back then. Later he would teach me again in the high school in Montevallo. He made twenty dollars per month and was a big influence on me. He was kind and seemed to know his stuff. I learned a lot about geography from him.

I liked the Nevins Place even better than the others. It was 120 acres with a big creek running along the west and north sides, which made for good hunting and fishing. I had learned to swim when I was six, so Mom didn't worry about me drowning in the big creek, though, if she had known about the water moccasins and rattle snakes we scared up every now and then, she might have.

Dad went to Iowa for work, picking corn, which was ever-so-tall there. Us kids had to fetch wood quite often. I learned how to harness and hook the horses to the wagon so I could go to the timber and get it. It was hard at first, but I soon got the hang of it. I was ten years old at that time. I was too short to get the harnesses and yokes over their heads, so I had to stand on a stool. I also began steering the plow behind them at about this age. Needless to say, I developed a strong back, arms, and hands. Milking cows every day by hand also added to that strength, which would serve me well later on in life. It was at this place that I learned to trap rabbits and hunt squirrels, which were both good to eat. I used traps that caught them live. I loved the timber!

When my dad was gone, I had many jobs. In addition to getting wood for the next day (no matter the weather) I had to milk the cows and feed the pigs and chickens, all which had to be done before I went to school. My brother, Virgil, was only two and a half, so Mom couldn't help me much with my work because he, along with all the housework, kept her pretty busy. We lived in the Nevins Place for two years and got flooded out both years. We lost 80 percent of our crops. That was when my mom and dad decided it was time to march to higher ground.

I knew that when we moved from the Nevins Place I would miss many things, like nuts and berries along the creek and also my swimming hole and the frog pond. But I chose to believe that the next place would be even better, and that made moving not so bad. Mr. Flynn, our mailman, liked Mom a lot. When he told us he had a nice farm to rent, we went to see it and liked it a lot.

Moving was always a big event. It was hard work, slow, and stressful and required all hands-on deck to help. It was 1928 now, and the night before the move, I could hardly wait for morning. When I looked outside, both our neighbors, Ray Blitzer and George Schoanweather, were there with their horses and wagons to help us. We loaded everything we owned, tied the cows behind the wagon, pushed the hogs and pigs into a box, and put the chickens into crates on the wagon. I would drive the horses with a click of the tongue and a feeling of pride that I could help out like an adult.

We made sure to take Betty, our sow pig, because she was more than a family pet. She had a litter of thirteen piglets every year. We always had to raise the runt on a bottle because she only had twelve tits. The funny thing was that the runt always ended up being the biggest one. We usually kept two of her piglets to eat later and sold the other eleven for between two and five dollars each. Betty deserved a good place on the wagon because of her predictable pregnancies!

My parents and Goldie and Virgil went ahead in the car so they could set up the stoves and have supper ready when the rest of us got there. When we took off, I drove the third wagon—our family wagon and horse. They placed my wagon in the middle because I was only around ten years old and I certainly didn't know where we were headed. I rode about twenty miles sitting on a sack of corn-cobs as a seat. I don't think I sat down for a day or two after that trip because my bottom was so sore.

The roads were muddy the entire way, and there was no gravel on the roads in those days. We got to our new house, the Flynn Place, around dark, and boy were we ready to eat! We unloaded the wagons and herded the animals into their separate pens. I helped feed and water them; they had been on a hard trip, too. At that point, we still had our mustang horses, Bess and Molly. Bess had become my horse, and we were used to each other by now.

The Flynn Place, our sixth tenant farm, included 160 acres of ground with only ten acres of timber. However, there was a lot of timber to the north of the farm. Because I had started to hunt and trap by now, I could tell it would be a good place for a lot of animals to live and, therefore, good for our family. I was ready to go and pretty excited about this new place.

The country store where we shopped for groceries was named Porshie and was only one-and-a-half miles away. El Dorado Springs, Missouri, was five and a half miles away, and Dedric was five miles away. Nevada was twelve miles away. We went to the country store when we walked or drove the horses and wagon. It was more convenient, and I liked going there because I could see a lot of different people.

Mom would only buy necessities like flour and sugar. As often as not, she would trade with the store owner, Tom Stockstill. She would swap our eggs for whatever she needed that day. It was a good way for us to get stuff at the store when we didn't have any money. One day, Mr. Stockstill gave me my first bottle of pop, an Orange Crush. What a day that was for me! George Jackson, Art Biddlecome, and Mr. Kennedy hung out in there, too. They were all farmers I knew who lived around me. They all knew I lived in hard circumstances and always treated me with respect and kindness. They treated me like I was one of them ... which I was.

Chapter 3

School, Work, and Money at the Flynn Farm

SCHOOL WAS A little better here, as we lived only a quarter of a mile away, across the plowed field. First days were always the worst, and once again I had to explain to the new teacher why my older sister, Goldie, was in the same grade as me: she had been sick and couldn't attend one year. At this point, I was beginning to understand that her sickness had changed her forever and that she was not able to learn like other kids. Since it was late March, I knew I only had to be in classes for less than a couple of months. Then I could be out for the summer. We only had eight-month terms then so kids could help in the fields in the spring and summer.

That summer, I learned to work in the fields. Dad had stepped on a rusty nail and couldn't walk. I wonder now if he had been infected with a case of tetanus. While he was healing, I plowed the ground with Bess and Molly and got it ready to plant crops. I would have been about ten or eleven years old, going on eleven, at that time. I had to stand on a bucket to get the harnesses and yoke over their heads. I had learned how to harness them from my step-dad. All of the machinery was horse-drawn, and I walked behind the horse and plow. Only the richer people could afford riding machinery, which was starting to replace horse-drawn machinery at that point, and that certainly didn't include our family.

A lady named Emma Jackson used kids to pick her blackberries every summer, so I had a chance to earn money at her place. She paid me two cents per quart, so I could make around forty to fifty cents each day if I started at daylight and worked until around noon. One day, Emma asked me to go with her to help sell and deliver the berries. We rode in her Model A to the small towns around us, like Walker and Shell City. I got to see all the sites, plus make a little extra money in the process. It was a long day but a fun one. At the time, I didn't understand why her son, Alvin, never picked with me or even helped her sell the berries. After all, he wasn't sick or feeble. He was about my age. That was a mystery I never solved.

My job was to take a quart of berries to the door of the house and ask the woman of the house if she wanted some. Usually they agreed to buy some, and Emma paid me twenty-five cents for helping all afternoon. That was a lot of money to me. I really wanted a bicycle, but I knew the money I earned was needed much more for other things for the family. The truth is, as I look back at this, it was the first time I saw that doing something other than working hard with my hands at trapping or farming could result in making money. It was my first experience at salesmanship, which would come in handy later in my life.

A very hot summer passed slowly until school started. Emma asked me if I would like to do janitor work at the school. Her husband, George, was a school board member and could influence the right people if I wanted the job. Mom thought I was too young, but I convinced her I could do it if they gave me the job.

My job was to keep the floors clean and oil them once a month, wash the windows when needed, and keep the fire alive in the stove in the cold weather. When the weather started getting colder, I would get up early and go to school to get the fire going and then come back home, eat breakfast, and get ready for school. Once a month, I would ride my horse to Mr. Hawkins's house and pick up my pay, three dollars for a month's work. He was not a nice man and one time even made me stand in the rain outside to get my pay instead of inviting me in where it was dry. I then rode back home and gave the check to Mom. She would need the money for groceries or other necessities.

I now knew a little about trapping rabbits, and I learned how to set a snare. On weekends my friend Lester Kennedy and I would dig out skunks and possums. We got $1.50 for skunks and possums; rabbits were ten cents each. In one season, I could catch four or five skunks and two or three possums. My dog, Gyp, helped me get lots of rabbits. One time, I lost eighty rabbits to a hot day in late fall; they all spoiled in the heat. I had waited too long to sell them. I learned a hard lesson from that experience, mainly that I wouldn't always make a profit from my work and that I needed to be very careful about protecting my hard work and not wasting it. I have applied that lesson throughout my life, and it has worked out pretty well for me. "Waste not want not", as the old expression goes.

People in town would eat the rabbits, but others used the animals for furs. It was a good way to make extra money, and I liked doing it. I sold larger quantities of my animals to a guy who resold them to people in Kansas City. He bought animals from me and the other kids who trapped. We knew he would sell them for even more money in Kansas City, but it was okay with us because we had a cash buyer.

A final bit of information about living at the Flynn Place: This was the beginning of the Depression and also the dry years—the beginning of the unforgiving drought of the '30s. We lost all of our cattle except one cow during that time period. I, unfortunately, caught a case of typhoid fever the same year that my brother Donald was born. It was in September 1929, the year of the great stock market crash. Even harder times followed.

Mom fed me a lot of chicken broth during that time. I couldn't eat because I was delirious for a long period, so she had to force-feed me. I believe she saved my life. I remember her putting cold compresses on my forehead and playing soothing songs on the piano. I was very weak when I finally came out of the sickness, but I survived thanks to my mother.

I remember coming home from school one day and my mom talking about Wall Street crashing. It must have been near the end of the 1920s. I was not yet a teenager, and I had not had any worldly experiences. I could only imagine that the buildings on Wall Street had all fallen down. Little did I know that this would be the start of many bad years, ones with even less money than we had already experienced.

The truth is that I sure hated moving from the Flynn Place. I liked my friends there and my jobs, too. If we had stayed longer, I would have been close to the high school. I had to give up my dog and all my friends to go to the land of nothing again. Watching my horse, Bess, being sold was the hardest part of this move. I had ridden her everywhere, and believe me, she could outrun all of the other horses in the neighborhood. I was always pretty proud of her. But, like before, it was time to move on. We had a sale and sold everything we owned for $310. Dad bought a 1924 Model T and away we went to Emerson, Nebraska. My brother, Donald, was only a few days old when we took off. As it turned out, moving from the Flynn Place was a big mistake, and the following years would tell that tale.

I had to leave my friends Webster, Raymond, and Alvie behind. I had four or five kids in my grade level in seventh grade in the one-room schoolhouse. I would once again have to make new friends in a new place where we would start all over from scratch again. In the land of nothing.

Chapter 4

Growing Up Was Hard at the Emerson Farm

WE ARRIVED AT Emerson, our seventh farm, southwest of Sioux City, Iowa, in late September 1929. We stayed with our supposed friend, Oscar Boyd, who had lived near our place in Missouri. He was a bachelor, and I could tell he had a crush on Mom. She slapped him one day in our kitchen when he made an impolite advance. He was the person who had told Dad there was work in Nebraska, which turned out to be false.

In early October, before corn-picking time, Dad worked for Oscar in a produce place where he bought and sold poultry and animal hides. Oscar was fair to Dad, paying him about a dollar a day until corn picking started in late October. Thinking he could make more money, Dad went to work picking corn out in the country. Since it meant he had to work from daybreak until dark, he was only home on Sundays. He had to sleep at the farms where he picked during the week.

Before I went to school here, I told Mom I would rather quit than have to go to school with Goldie. I was not willing to be made fun of for her behavior and learning issues. I knew now that other kids could recognize her retardation, and it really bothered me. Mom agreed, and Goldie never went to school again. I convinced Mom it was too much for me to take her to school because of all my other demands.

In winter she couldn't go, anyhow. She was always unsteady on her feet.

The new school was a lot different from my others. Each grade had a separate room and teacher. All the kids seemed real friendly at first. I was in the seventh grade, and I can't remember the name of my teacher there because I was only there for about three months. But I do remember that I learned a lot in the short time I was there. I memorized Europe's and South America's capital cities, and I still can recite most of them today. I could tell that my school in Missouri had not made me fall behind these kids. I was even better at math then they were. For one reason or another, the teacher liked me. Even though I would later experience bullying on the playground, the teacher made sure there was none of that in the classroom. It was a safe place for me. Earl Jadlow and his gang of buddies loved bullying me because I was from Missouri, and they thought people from Missouri were hillbillies.

Our stoves at Emerson Farm burned coal, and there was a railroad station about a quarter of a mile south. The train stopped there and fueled up, and the coal cars always lost a little coal, so we went there to pick it up and bring it home to burn in the stove. The truth is that we also stole a lot of coal. It seemed okay to us boys, as we watched adult men doing it, too. Train workers even felt sorry for us kids and sometimes threw some off the railroad cars so we could have it.

When the weather was good, I would make several trips each night, and I was accumulating a pretty big pile. So I thought about selling some. In the three months we were there, I sold twelve dollars worth of coal for fifty cents a bushel. With the profits, I bought a wagon to haul the coal. With my wagon, I could now get kindling for our fires that I found behind the stores on the way home, as they threw out their cardboard and wood crates. It seemed like I had a real business now. This experience turned out to be another good one in teaching me how to build a business and reinvest my money in that business. That self-taught lesson would become important to me later on when I started my first construction business.

In mid-November, Mom came down with a sore throat, which back then they called quinsy. She was in bed for two weeks and almost died. My youngest brother, Donald, was only a few weeks old, and Virgil was less than four years old. Someone had to take care of them, so I had to stay home from school to keep the house warm. I also had to wash the dirty diapers and clothes. We had no washing machine, and I had to use a washboard.

Mom finally got well, and Dad came home from picking corn, and we had a long winter ahead. Dad had no jobs, and Mom said, "We're leaving this place." She had written to his folks in Oklahoma and told them we would be coming down to stay with them. I was glad to leave the Emerson school, too, because by now the guys had started making fun of me, calling me a Missouri hillbilly. I didn't know how to react and could have told them that I had been born just across the state line in Iowa to shut them up. But I didn't have the sense to do that then.

So we loaded the car and away we went before Dad's earnings, $175, ran out. No one could sell anything at that time, so we left what little we had in the house, except for the clothes and bedding we could pack. It was January by now, and the ride to Oklahoma was a cold one. It was pretty hard on my brothers because they were so young. It was rough on Mom, too, as she had just gotten well from her sickness.

Chapter 5

Back to Oklahoma

WE ARRIVED AT the Dr. Pope ranch in the middle of January. It was our eighth place to live since Mom remarried, and boy were we glad for the warmer weather in Oklahoma. There were three houses on the ranch, and my dad's folks lived in the one that was about a quarter mile from the big ranch house. We stayed there until spring and then moved into the little house across the road from the big ranch house. Our place was a three-room tarpaper shack with one bedroom. Back then a lot of houses had tarpaper on the outside as the only covering. We thought it was normal.

Charlie Robinson, my step-cousin who had early-on befriended me, was the only person working. He worked for Jessie Pope, the woman who ran the whole ranch. The doctor had died some years back, and no one else in the family could find work. It was the beginning of the Depression and anyone would do any work they could find, like Dad going to Iowa or Nebraska to pick corn in the fall. In the cities like Kansas City there was no work. Dad told me there were mile-long lines of people for the few jobs that became available and also to get bread and food. Our mother would have never allowed us to stand in a food line. She was too proud and somehow always put some kind of food on the table. We ate a lot of flour, milk or water, and bacon grease biscuits to make it through the winters.

Charlie got twenty-five dollars a month, plus room and board, and he bought my books so I could start school again. I'll never forget that. I went to the Wizenhaun school there, and my teacher was Marie Lite. All the kids there were as poor or even poorer than us. I was ahead of them in schoolwork, so I guess I learned a lot at Emerson in the short time I attended there. There were only about five or six white kids in this school. The rest were Indians. Most of them seemed old for their grades. My new friend, a girl named Elsie Austin, was later raped by her father. I heard he went to the penitentiary because of it. He got what he deserved. She was a nice girl.

School was just part of my busy days. That first winter in Oklahoma, I got up at 5:00 a.m. to milk the cows at the dairy they ran on the ranch. They also had range cattle, so I had to feed them hay in the winter months. After milking and feeding hay, I ate breakfast and went to school, which was only a mile and a half away. After school, it was back to milking and feeding hay. But after supper I got to hunt for possums and coons. I was able to get $1.50 per possum and $2.50 to $7.50 for a coon pelt. I learned how to follow the leads of my two hound dogs and made good money that year. I caught seven or eight possums and one to two coons. That money, of course, went to help with my family's finances.

During the summer, I made extra money by helping in the hay fields. I was only about eleven years old, and I had to learn how to move hay with a bull rake and hay bailer. By now I had gotten pretty good with horses and mules. One day, my auth Jessie sent me to fetch some shingles eight miles away with the mules and a wagon. I got home after dark, and I thought it was the biggest thing I had ever done! Jesse thought I was lost or hurt and came looking for me. She shined a light on my wagon, and I could see that she had been worried about me. She followed me home after intercepting me to make sure I got there all right. At the time, I hadn't had enough sense to understand the danger of the situation, I was just feeling grown-up.

That summer I made fifty cents a day working in the fields, and I was pretty proud of myself. I dreamed over and over about the many ways I would ever be able to spend that much money. That bicycle I had always wanted was on that list. As it turned out, I never got to spend any of it, as Dad always needed it for medical bills for health problems Mom started having or other family bills.

We lived near Oolagah, Oklahoma, the birthplace of Will Rogers. I didn't know anything about him or that he was famous or a comedian or political satirist or anything then. I don't think I had even heard a radio yet, so I hadn't heard his program of political humor and commentary. I just remember one day when Charlie took me to a movie and then to a pool hall in Oolagah, he told me that Will Rogers was there. I didn't go up and talk to him, but now I wish I had.

During the winter of 1930, our whole family, except me, had diphtheria, and we were quarantined, which meant we could not leave house for several days. I had to sneak out to help with the milking and feeding. I was just too busy to be able to help care for the sick people in my house. Dr. Bushyhead came out from Claremore, Oklahoma, and gave us all antitoxin shots. I didn't need one, but he gave me one anyway, and the reaction really made me cramp for about six hours, but by morning I was able to go milk. Donald was only fifteen months old, and Virgil was just five years old. Since everyone had the disease, I couldn't go to school during the day, so I had more time for myself. I went hunting with the hounds, Sythe and Sue, when the weather permitted. I really enjoyed this and was able to make even more money from my furs during that absence from school. Like any kid, I didn't mind missing a little school.

The house our grandparents—my step-grandparents, John and Caldonia Robinson—lived in burned down, and they moved across the Verdigris River about four miles from the ranch. I rode a little mule over there one day and had to cross the river and big lake, not knowing that some mules can't swim, I think because their hooves are too small. I almost lost my mule. I slid off her back and grabbed her tail, and we finally made it across, both coughing and shivering on the shoreline. January makes for a pretty cold swim. I never crossed that river with my mule again. I guess my guardian angel was with me, as he would be many more times later on in life. Anyway, when I went home, I took the road for six or eight miles.

Winter came and went, and the cows started having calves. The dairy calves had to be hand-fed, so Jessie told Dad that for every five calves he raised, he could have one. We took care of twenty-five calves that summer, so I got one of Dad's five calves because I had taken care of them all anyway. Later, Dad traded my calf for a cow that didn't produce good milk; she made lumpy milk. He sold the cow for five dollars and used the money to pay bills. I never got that money either. But I did get to dream about spending it. I looked at bicycles in the Sears catalogue and thought about how great it would be to have one. I never owned a bike and don't know how to ride one to this day, but I did help my little brothers buy their first bikes with some of my earnings.

Once a year they herded cattle into big corrals for branding and dehorning. My job on Jesse's place was to go out and find cattle and bring them to the corral. That summer I learned to rope calves and do everything you do on a cattle horse. The ranch had a horse called Jim. He was a tall, fast seven-year-old coral-colored gelding with three white feet. That horse knew more about cattle than I did. I sure missed him when we moved back to Missouri later that year.

My grandmother who lived in Iowa died in summer of 1931. My parents went to the funeral and were gone about ten days. I had to stay home and take care of things. They made the trip in the 1921 Model T Ford in the hotter part of the summer.

My dad had planted about twenty acres of corn on the other side of the Verdigris River, about two miles from the ranch. While he was gone, I crossed the river with a team of mules and a cultivator and tilled the corn. When my folks came home, they were really surprised. My mom said she would have never let me cross that river, but it wasn't as bad as she thought; the water was shallow in one spot.

This about covers the highlights of Oklahoma, except for my friend, Elsie Austin. We would also walk behind a kid called Son Clark and pick up the orange peelings he would throw away. We were embarrassed to be eating the peels, but we really liked them, and we promised each other never to tell anyone. We were always hungry, and those orange peels tasted pretty doggone good on an empty stomach. I missed her friendship after our move.

I also liked hunting with a boy called Swinten Pittman, who had a little sister called Verna Lee. Sometimes, I would go with my uncles Claude, Charlie, and Jess and Bill Robinson to play cards, mostly pitch, at the neighbor's house; the neighbors' names were Crist Huggit and Bob Clark. My other uncles Jim and George were older and not around much.

These experiences kept me happy, and I never realized the harsh severity of my family's situation because I had lots of people around me going through the same thing. And my new step-relatives had accepted me as one of their own. For that I am forever grateful.

Chapter 6

The Depression deepens, Garret Place

1933: AT THE AGE OF THIRTEEN or fourteen, my seventh-grade year in school, we moved from Okalahoma to the Garret Place, our ninth tentant farm, five and a half miles east of Milo Frazier School.

That was in November of 1931. I was really sad to be leaving the other Robinsons, especially my step-uncle Charlie. We brought our calves and chickens in a four-wheeled trailer pulled behind the old Model T. Two of Dad's brothers brought the furniture.

I started seventh grade at the Milo Frazier School. A male teacher taught there, and his mode of punishment involved long switches. The school had a lot of kids. We had to sit two and three in a seat. I was sitting by the window one day, and a boy named Delbert Woods reached across and spit tobacco out the window. Since I was by the window, when the teacher saw tobacco juice, he assumed I was responsible. I was made to go to the front and take my punishment. I was afraid of Delbert at that time, so I didn't tell on him.

A student could choose from different kinds of punishment, depending on the teacher. Some of them included putting your nose in a circle drawn on the blackboard, standing in a corner, staying after school, or the switching or spanking. I would rather take the switching so I could get it over quicker. If a woman teacher had a big boy she could not handle, she would call an official of the district, which didn't happen too often. This particular teacher laid into me pretty good, but I still kept my mouth shut because of Delbert.

About all I had to do that winter was take care of calves, hunt at night, and keep Mom in wood while Dad was away picking corn in Iowa. By picking corn, I mean taking the mature dried-out cob off the stalk and filling bushel baskets. They didn't have mechanical reapers at this time, and the corn was "picked" by hand. The Depression was really getting bad. Everyone was out of work, and being raised in a poor part of the country didn't help much. We should have stayed in Oklahoma. At least I was making a little money there, and there was always something to do on the ranch to make even a little more, like hunting rabbits.

We stayed on the Garret Place that winter and in the spring moved about three and a half miles east to our tenth tenant farm, to the Frank Smith Place in 1933–1934. I was between the ages thirteen to fifteen. We moved rather aburbtly to the Frank Smith Place, six-and-a half-miles west of Montevallo, twelve miles southeast of Nevada, Missouri, our tenth farm. I think Mom thought the pastures would be greener there. It didn't take us long to find out we were surrounded by dry land and dust as far as the eye could see in every direction.

That put us in the Round Prairie school district, about one-and-a-quarter miles from the Nevins' place, where I had gone to school when I was eight and nine years old. Being thirteen years old and more grown up now, I knew how to do things better, or should I say more efficiently, such as fishing. I could make a seine out of burlap sacks to catch fish. I also had my own dog for hunting game. I could catch more fish in fifteen minutes with the seine than I could catch all day with a hook and line. I have never liked fishing, ever since my boyhood. It always seemed like a chore. Fishing was never fun to me. It wasn't fun when my family needed what I gathered to survive. That just sapped the fun right out of it for me.

I got a job that first summer working for Frank Fenten, who was an automobile body and fender repairman in Nevada. He owned a farm about a mile and a half from us, so it wasn't far to walk. My job that summer was tearing out old fence, building new fence, and cleaning up fence lines covered in brush, blackberry vines, poison oak, and whatever else grew there. It could reach about 105 to 112 degrees during that dry summer, which made for one scorching-hot job. I made fifty cents a day the first summer. I asked for half day off to go to the Labor Day parade toward the end of the summer, and Fenton took off fifteen cents from my pay that day. If I had known he would do that, I would not have gone. I was more upset with myself than I was him.

At this point, I had been in four schools in three different states. I attended the eighth grade two years in a row because I couldn't afford the new books or clothes for high school. Repeating the eighth grade gave me more time to make enough money. No one explained to me that I could buy used books. I figured that out after my second year of eighth grade. When I was getting ready to buy the used books, the teacher gave me the books himself. He must have recognized my situation and decided to help me.

Winter came, and a man named McMinnis who was hard of hearing and had three coonhounds needed someone to go with him at night who could hear when they treed a coon. He offered me half of the profit, and I will never know if I got my fair share. My job was to climb the tree and scare the raccoons down so the dogs could kill them. One night I was about twenty-five feet up in a tree and I went out on a limb that I didn't know was dead. It broke and I hit the ground with the coons, dogs, and all with McMinnis hollering at me to see if I was alright. I guess that's that guardian angle I was talking about earlier. I never even got a scratch.

We did pretty well that winter. One night we had three coons up one tree and I got two of them. That old Indian taught me a lot about hunting and trading and also how to shoe a horse. He showed me how to judge the quality of furs and how to ask for more money for the best ones. I knew the fur buyers from the city had taken advantage of us boys. McMinnis taught me how to make groups of furs and sell them together to make more money. I learned from him how to make as much profit out of a deal as possible and how to judge quality.

I graduated from eighth grade in 1932. There wasn't much to graduating in the Depression years. No one had money for the fancy things of today. The country schools all gathered at a large church for the graduation ceremony, and there were only four to six students from each school. None of us had suits or ties, so we just wore a sweater and jeans to graduation.

The second year we lived on the Smith Place, I worked for my stepuncle John Wells, who had married Dad's sister Lettie. He was building a country store, which would later be called the Sandstone Store. He had bought an old hotel in Pitcher, Oklahoma, and I helped him haul the lumber in an old Model A truck. It took all summer. That old country store would be my hangout for the rest of my teen years. My stepuncle was an ex-boxer, and he taught me about boxing and how to fight. Young kids and some older ones would gather on Sunday afternoons, and the matches would sometimes go on for two or three hours. I didn't have to worry much about bullies after that. I took care of myself very well. I found out that my strength and fighting skills matched up pretty well with the other young men in the area.

In the fall of 1934, I started attending high school at Montevallo, Missouri. It was six and a half miles to walk or ride a horse from the Smith Place. In bad weather and when it was really cold, I would walk. My horse had to be outside all day when I rode him to school. He would run loose and when I was ready to go home at the end of the day, he was never too far away. My horse, Pat, was half Thoroughbred and half bronco/mustang. I got him when he was young and broke him myself. He was my buddy, and we really got to know each other. There are those who do not and cannot understand the relationship between a hores and a man. But Pat was a soul-mate.

There were only about twenty houses in town. At the start of the school year, there were about fifty students. By Christmas there were only about thirty or less because the girls stayed home when the weather turned bad. Some of them got jobs from people in town and worked as live-in housekeepers. The city folks took advantage of them because they could, times being what they were, pay them almost nothing.

There were no school buses until 1937, so making the hike to and from school was pretty rough on the girls and some of the boys. The old high school had two rooms, one upstairs and one downstairs. In the morning, the first- and second-year students were downstairs and the juniors and seniors were upstairs. In the afternoon we switched places. My classes were civil government, algebra, English literature, general science, physical education, and agriculture.

We learned about terracing that year and how to farm in good and bad weather. The government, through the Agricultural Adjustment Act, better known as the AAA, had started these kind of learning programs in school to make people aware of the erosion that was occurring because of the great drought during the Depression, how ignorance of plowing and planting methods added to the dust bowl misery, and how we might manage the land smarter to avoid those problems in the future. It was one of FDR's government programs that really made a difference in how farmers, especially young ones like us, would treat the land with more respect and wisdom in future generations.

We had outdoor toilets and an old well. We got our drinking water from the well. Our basketball court was outside and had a top layer of cinders, which were the ashes from the old coal stoves. If you fell while playing you lost a little hide. The year before I started high school the team won the state championship. The school never had a good team after that. I played on the basketball team until I left for the Civilian Conservation Corps (CCC Camp) at the end of my sophomore year.

From 1934 to 1937 would be the worst years of the Depression. No rain came either, which caused the Dust Bowl. The grasshoppers ate all the vegetation. I set steel traps between home and school during trapping season and checked them on my way home from school. I never caught much, but what I did catch helped my family survive some pretty tough times, as money was scarce.

While living on the Smith Place, I learned how to make whisky, which Mom called moonshine. Jerry Stokes paid me a little to help him guard his place when he was away. He later fell off a load of hay and died; there went my part-time job. I learned how to manipulate a cooker with a system of copper coils that dripped a slow stream of sugar, corn chops, and the finished moonshine through ice water and into a bucket. All the sheriffs bought their moonshine from my dad. I delivered the finished product to Leslie Hunt, the head officer. Without the money from moonshine, we would have gone to bed hungry more often than we did. It brought in much-needed cash and was more profitable than selling the corn itself.

We moved to West Place, our eleventh tenant farm, in March 1933. It was about the same distance from school, a little over six miles. We had traded for a team of mules that were too big to ride, so I had to walk, but by the time I reached school, eight or ten kids had usually joined me, so I had company. To make things worse, we had a really bad winter in the mid 1930s, with lots of very cold temperatures and snow. The kids who walked with me included: James Hamilton, his friend Rusty Haynes, Nadine Grant, and Ruth Wheeler. Nadene Grant was a knockout, and I was sweet on her, but she had a boyfriend and stuck with him. Ruth Wheeler was my girlfriend on the side, but she had a steady boyfriend, too. She was also a beautiful young lady. I lived the farthest away, so they all waited on me to show up before they set out, and we all watched out for each other.

We didn't have warm clothes like people have today because we had no money to buy them. We were in the worst of the Depression at this point. There was no rain in summer, the winters were cold, and we had no money or jobs. I set traps and hunted at night with dogs, but I didn't have much luck. I caught rabbits and squirrels on weekends, to eat. I missed my two Treeing Walker Coonhounds, Syth and Sue, that I had hunted with in Oklahoma. They had helped me catch a lot of other animals besides just coons. They had easily treed squirrels and scared rabbits out of hiding.

Chapter 7

Civilian Conservation Corps Camp

I WAS NEARLY sixteen years old when I heard about the Civilian Conservation Corps (CCC) camps for young men. President Franklin Roosevelt established the CCC for families with no income, which at that time included about 90 percent of the population. The boys were paid thirty dollars a month, five dollars of which they got to keep and the rest of which was sent home to help their families survive desperate times.

I signed up in December 1933. My mother did not want me to go because it was in the middle of my sophomore year of high school. I didn't have much hope of being called, but to my surprise, two months later, in February 1934, I got a notice in the mail to report at the courthouse in Nevada, Missouri. But I still had two rivers to cross. First, I had to convince the doctor that I was eighteen years old. Second, I had to prove that being born with a lazy eye which allowed my left eye only fuzzy vision wasn't a handicap. Fortunately, neither would prove to be an issue. My eye had never bothered me or hindered me from doing anything I wanted, and I had always looked older than my age. They didn't even ask for my birth certificate.

Later in my life, though, that eye kept me from getting some good jobs. Maybe that was for the best because I ended up working for myself later in life, which required no physical exam. Besides, I had never thought of the lazy eye as a handicap; it never kept me from being a good boxer or hindered me in any way, except when people judged me as incompetent or unhirable for it.

The CCC camp sent me to Chesapeake, Missouri about thirty miles east of Carthage in March 1934. The camp looked and was run like the army, except there were no guns. I liked camp life. We got good food and clothes and five dollars a month spending money. We worked in the fields eight hours a day, building a fish hatchery, in what we called hell on earth, with temperatures high as 116 degrees Fahrenheit. We didn't have heat index back then. Hot was hot and sweat was sweat.

We dug the holes and graded the dirt with picks and shovels. Because there were not many machines, we did most of the work by hand, and the younger boys like me got all the hard jobs. Being the youngest out of 265 men and boys, I was at the bottom of the heap. We carried water to the fields in ten-gallon milk cans. The crew leader, a real bully everyone called Copperknob, was supposed to have two different boys carry the cans each morning, but he decided he didn't like me, so I never got to change off with a second carrier. I had a real problem with respecting authority at that point in my life, especially the authority of a person like Copperknob.

I had an older friend at the camp named Murray Haines who was also a leader over another group of boys. He noticed what was going on and told me I didn't need to do that every morning. So the next morning when Copperknob told me to carry the milk can of water, I refused to do it.

When we got to the job, he came over and said, "I'll see you down at the spring after supper." The spring was the place we hung out at after work. He was redheaded, had one crossed eye, and was around twenty-five years old. He also outweighed me by about forty or fifty pounds.

Being just a kid, I was scared out of my socks, but my friend Murray from back home assured me that I could whip him and tried to tell me how to do it. When the camp heard there was going to be a fight, they all came to watch.

I had been waiting there for about ten minutes when all of a sudden he came running straight at me. All I could do was try! He had his eyes shut as he ran, so I cracked him one punch right in the eye, grabbed him around the neck, and was too scared to let loose. When he started turning black and blue, Murray pulled me off him and said, "I told you you could whip him."

Boy, was I glad that was over, but I think a higher power had an angel helping that day guide my fist to that closed eye and show me a strength I had no idea I possessed in that exact moment. Anyway, I became the most popular young man in that CCC camp overnight.

The ambulance hauled both of us back to camp and into the army captain's office. He looked at both of us, kind of smirked, and said, "I think you got the worst of it," to Copperknob.

Since Copperknob was a leader with three stripes, he got busted back to working in the gang and was robbed of his authority over the recruits. I hadn't been in camp long enough to have a rank, so I had nothing to lose. We were both given forty extra hours of duty, so I headed straight to the mess hall to start mine.

When I got there, the mess sergeant wanted to know why I was there and what I had done. At about that time Copperknob came in with his black eye and the mess sergeant set him to washing dishes. I was put in the back and was peeling potatoes when the sergeant came back to tell me to go out the back door and that my forty hours were considered done. I found out from that experience that no one likes a bully. Copperknob was the camp champ in that department, and everybody knew it.

That was the only trouble I had all summer, and it all turned out for the best. I never carried a milk can of water again all summer, either.

I soon finished my six months of CCC duty. While I had enjoyed my stay at the camp, I hadn't liked the unbearable heat and the hot sun. They were pretty tough on us younger ones, giving us the hardest jobs, as I mentioned before. But it toughened me up.

On weekends we went to other camps and had boxing matches. I was one of the better boxers in our unit, mostly because no one I boxed there was tougher than the old boys I boxed from back home. When we had bouts with the other camps, I fought at 135 pounds, and we had three-round matches. My opponents mostly tired out and quit before the fights were over. We often sparred in my own camp, and I could seldom find guys in my weight class who would box me. I always had to fight up a couple weight classes, but I still won most of the matches.

We could also go into town (Aurora or Mount Vernon) on the weekends in the army truck, but there was not much to do. We could have more fun playing games like pool, ping-pong, horseshoes, or boxing at the camp, which was good for entertainment. Sometimes we paired up and went hiking in the hills. I had never had "days off" before in my life because farm work was pretty much 24-7, so I really liked weekends at the CCC camp. It was like play to me. Often I would take other guys KP (Kitchen Patrol) duty to make extra money because playing all weekend seemed like a waste of time to me.

Emery Carl Hinkhouse, Jr.

    I liked the camp but missed my high school friends, especially my girlfriend, so when August came, I wrote her a letter and had her ask our teacher if I could come back and start my new year and make up the year I had missed. Two weeks later I got a letter saying to come on back. He told me they needed me for the basketball team.

Chapter 8

First Trip to Minnesota

I GOT MY discharge papers and arrived home in time for the first day of school in September. I had made enough money to buy a two-year-old riding horse for myself. So now I had it to ride to school when the weather was good. The horse had not been broken yet, so I broke him myself and taught him the ropes, so to speak. Riding him to school and back was a good way to teach him. He learned really fast and was a very smart horse who was easy to ride and seemed to be able to read commands from my mind.

One evening when we were coming home from school, the young horse, being green and very high-strung, jumped up onto a wet wooden bridge so fast that his feet slid out from under him. He fell on top of me and dragged all the skin off one of my ankles and broke the bone. I was on crutches for six weeks or so. When I was healed to the point that I only needed one crutch, one morning when we were playing chinny before school, my schoolmate Walter hit my other ankle with his club. My crutches came back for another six weeks.

Chinny was played like hockey only we used a tin can as a puck and everyone made his own club out of whatever tree branch or board they could manage to hit with. After about thirty minutes, the tin can was the size of a walnut.

I later realized that my broken ankles had been a blessing in disguise. I had always had trouble with sprained ankles before that, but after having two broken ankles at about the same time, I have not had a bad ankle since.

We moved from West Place in the spring of 1935 to a place about eight miles east of Nevada, Missouri, called the 80X Acres. It was our eleventh tenant farm since Mom's second marriage to my stepdad. The move was about five miles. We took everything but the house furniture. It took all week to move everything with a team of mules and a wagon. I was two-thirds done with my junior year, and that was the end of my Montevallo High School days and walking or riding my horse six-and-a-half miles to and from school. The new place was ten miles from the high school. That was when I quit going to school. Ten miles was a long hike. I later finished my high school work at the CCC camp in Butler, Missouri.

That year, 1935, was much like 1934, only worse. We had moved to a new eighty-acre farm and that summer brought 112-degree temperatures, drought, dust blowing in from Kansas, and clouds of grasshoppers that ate everything and left nothing but bare ground in their wake. They even ate the fence posts and the wood siding from barns and houses because there were no crops for them to eat. Talk about adding misery to woe! This made life very unpleasant for the older people. I started tilling the ground for spring planting and at the same time thinking about whether I was going to finish my last year of high school or look for work.

That was when Mom's health started to get a lot worse. I decided I had better find work because the place we'd moved to did not have good prospects for profitable crops. I had to find something that brought in some money so I could help Mom. She got worse by the day, and my little brothers, Virgil and Donald, soon came down with the same thing she had. We didn't know at that time that my stepfather had brought a serious disease into the family, one that no one in the family at that time knew about.

I had been driving cows to the creek and hauling water because all the wells had gone dry. When I talked about leaving home, Dad sold all but one cow for five dollars apiece. He only had four or five. The cow he kept later starved to death during yet another year of drought and crop failure. There wasn't enough grain or hay to keep even one cow alive.

Times were pretty rough. Many people went to bed hungry and woke up hungry. If it had not been for the Works Progress Administration (WPA), the Public Works Administration (PWA), and the CCC, there would have been even more starvation, both animal *and* human. We were thankful for a good president—Franklin D. Roosevelt. He was born rich but had great compassion for poor and working-class people. He knew that the first thing people needed was food and without that, nothing else would work.

I decided to try to find work. I went to the bank in Milo, Missouri, because the man that ran it, Ben Hart, had watched me grow up and I thought he might loan me money for a bus ticket. When I told him what I was going to do, he went into the back and came back with ten dollars. He said if I ever got an extra ten dollars, I could send it to him. I'm pretty sure he gave me his own ten dollars, because he didn't ask me to sign a note or anything.

My mom cried for several days when she found out I was about to leave for a second time to help the family survive. She and my dad took me to Nevada, Missouri, and I bought a bus ticket. That left $1.65 from the ten dollars Mr. Hart had given me. I boarded the bus, and as it pulled away, the last thing I saw was my mom crying and my two little brothers, my sister, and my dad waving good-bye. All I had for clothes went in an old suitcase that was held closed by an old belt.

We hadn't gone very far before I wished I was back home, but the feeling soon wore off when we pulled into the Pickwick Hotel bus stop in Kansas City, Missouri. I had never seen so many people in all my life. As I sat in the station, waiting for my next bus, a fellow wanted me to go outside into an alley to watch a rooster fight, but even as dumb as I was, I was too smart for that. I knew he just wanted to rob me, and I would have none of that.

I finally got to St. James, Minnesota, sometime that night and sat in the bus station until morning. Then I called my Aunt Sadie and she came and got me. I stayed with her family for about a week or ten days, and I thought my Uncle, Russell Reddenbaugh, didn't like me. He would give me dirty looks when we ate together, as if he thought I was taking too much food. I never felt welcome there but more like an imposition to them. I took off on foot to look for a job and to get out of there. I stopped at every farm along the road, but it was a bit too early to do spring work and no one needed anything done.

Chapter 9

Finally, a Job!

I WALKED FOR about two days and was about ready to give up when I came to an old country church the on the second night. It was getting dark, so I walked up the steps and opened the door to the entryway. It was really warm because they had the fire going. I figured the most anyone could do if they came in was kick me out, but no one came in. When daylight came, I started out again. About six years later, I found out that Evelyn, my future wife, had been confirmed in that Lutheran church in Sveadahl, Minnesota, and that she lived close by.

I headed northwest from the church. Since the weather was pretty cold early in morning, I had to keep moving or freeze. I soon found out that I wasn't dressed for Minnesota weather in March. I later found out that Evelyn had a little brother buried in the cemetery behind the church where I had found refuge. I would meet and marry Evelyn six years later, but a lot happened in between.

Around about ten o'clock that morning, with much delight, I came to an old country store. Since I'd had nothing to eat but the shelled corn and grain I had found along the road, I was getting pretty lank. I went into the store and bought a five-cent Baby Ruth candy bar. Now I only had $1.60 left, but boy was that candy bar good, so good that I stretched it out all morning.

The man in the store told me about a man named Victor Bloom who might need someone to help on his farm. His farm was about two miles from the store, so I started out to find his place. I got there around sundown, and he said he didn't need anyone right then but that if I would work for nothing for six weeks, he would start paying me. I was pretty desperate, so I accepted his offer. He turned out to be the meanest man I ever worked for.

We would get up at 4:45 a.m. and work until 8:00 or 9:00 p.m. every night. On top of that, he would cuss at me. I had been working for him for about two and a half weeks when he called me a really bad name, so I quit and told him to pay me. His wife took my side and told him he hadn't treated me very well. I could see that she felt bad for me and knew all about her husband's sour disposition, which she was stuck with pretty doggone well. I ended up staying because she was nice and I didn't have any place else to go. After about eight weeks, he paid me for two and back down the road I hiked.

There is more than I can tell here about Victor Bloom, but here are some of the incidents that I remember well. One time I was walking to St. James to get a money-order for ten dollars to send to Ben Hart, the man who had loaned me the bus money. Mr. Bloom came along with his car and didn't even stop to pick me up. My cousin drove me back. That was the only time I was off Victor's place during the time I worked for him.

The night he hired me, it was late in the evening and they were eating supper. His wife asked if I had eaten. Being bashful and feeling awkward, I told them I already had. It wasn't really a lie; I just didn't say it had been three days ago. While they were eating supper, I went down to the milk house and barn where they kept the milk and cream. I drank a big amount of cream, and since I had not eaten for three days, it made me really sick, but I felt better by morning. At least I had gotten some much-needed food into my stomach.

We got up at 4:45 a.m. When I came downstairs, he had rolls and coffee, and then we went out and milked twelve cows, separated the milk, and then fed about sixty head of stock, cattle and 180 head of hogs. We then went in and ate breakfast, and then back out we went to clean out the stables because the animals had been kept in the barn all winter because of the severe winter in Minnesota that year. We had a fifteen-minute lunch around midmorning, a big meal at noon, another lunch in the midafternoon, a six o'clock supper, and coffee and rolls at nine thirty or ten o'clock. I wasn't accustomed to eating that much or that often, so I usually skipped the lunch. I soon got caught up on my eating. So if nothing else, I at least got my strength back at the Blooms' with all those food-filled days.

One other thing I found interesting was that the Swedes had different names for things. They called a harrow a drag. One day Mr. Bloom told me to hook four head of horses to the drag. I hooked the horses to the road drag, and when he came out, I was dragging the driveway. Boy, did he ever tell me off. I told him he should look in the machinery guide and see what they called them. His wife looked it up and told him I was right. I don't think it made much of an impression one him.

That covers just a few of the things that happened during the short time I worked for Victor Bloom. I began to wonder if everyone in Minnesota was like him. I soon found out otherwise.

That spring, I stayed with my other aunt, Clara, who we called Gran, for about three or four days. In May or June, I found a job helping put up the first cutting of alfalfa hay. I was getting $2.50 per day but had no board and room to pay. Boy! I had never made that much money before. It was almost dark when we quit for the night, and I would walk to town to find a bite to eat. I would go to a store and buy a loaf of bread and small can of meat and cookies, which lasted me until noon the next day.

Every three days I would walk the three miles to my aunt's house for a change of clothes. On the other nights I would skinny dip in the lake. I did that for a while. I was sleeping in the shed out by the barn. The farm owners caught me one morning and wanted to know why I hadn't told them I didn't have a place to stay. They insisted I stay in the house and eat with them. I told them I would eat with them but said I would rather sleep in the open shed because it was cooler out there. I also did not want to dirty another bed for them.

To make a long story at least a little shorter, I worked there for about two and a half weeks until hay season was over and then went two miles east of Ormsby, Minnesota, and got hired by a man named Gliden Tate. It was a little early for harvest, but he said I could work there for the rest of the summer and he would try to find something for me to do. He was the best man I had worked for so far. He would go somewhere in the morning and never tell me what to do. For about half the time, I was goofing off with his son, John Jr., and waiting for harvest to start. I think he was trying to let me be a kid as much as he could. He seemed sympathetic to my circumstances.

One of my duties on his farm was milking at night and in the morning. While I was doing that, I also taught their daughter to milk. When harvest time started, my job was to run a bundle wagon and haul the bundles. Her job was running the threshing machine. It was hard work, but I liked it. I liked her as a friend but not as a girlfriend. Sometimes you just know when there isn't a connection.

At that time, my cousin Marion "Tough" Bell was working for another man, doing the same thing. He was from Mapleton, Iowa. The man he was working for offered me eighty acres if I would work for him for ten years. I think he was trying to get me hooked up with his daughter. He was the richest farmer in the county. His name was Anderson, and he was a really nice man. I think all the other young fellows were a little jealous that he liked me, the backwoods Missouri boy.

I worked for Mr. Tate until early September, when I received a letter from my mom saying she was really sick and that I needed to come home because she could no longer take care of my sister and my little brothers. So I packed my suitcase and headed home. I knew my mom had to be pretty sick to call me home.

Emery Carl Hinkhouse Sr.
Emery Carl Hinkhouse Sr. and Hazel Stella Hinkhouse
Emery Carl Hinkhouse Sr.

Emery Carl Hinkhouse Jr.

Silas Stauffer and his registered Poland Hogs
Hazel, Sadie, and Clara Stauffer
Silas Stauffer with his son, George
Hazel Stella Stauffer Hinkhouse

Goldie & Emery Hinkhouse with half-
brothers, Virgil and Donald Robinson
Jess Stauffer with Donald and Emery
Emery Carl Hinkhouse Jr. tallest on in the back row

Emery in his late teens or early twenties.
Evelyn Nelson Hinkhouse at seventeen

Emery Jr. in his Civilian Conservation Corps uniform.
Emery
Emery

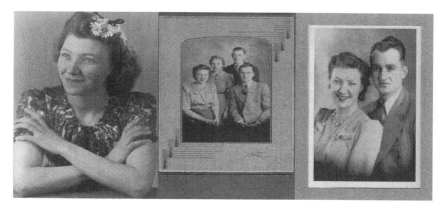

Evelyn Elvera Hinkhouse
Wedding pic of Evelyn and Emery with witnesses Harold
Nelson and his then girlfriend. Harold was killed in WW II.
Evelyn Elvera "Nelson" and Emery Carl Hinkhouse Jr.

**Early marriage
Joyce and Audrey Hinkhouse**

Alvin (Bud) Nelson, Evelyn, Joyce, Audrey
and Emery on Farm in Nevada Mo.
Hauling Flax straw

Emery in his Merchant Marines uniform with
Evelyn, Joyce, and Audrey Hinkhouse.
Emery's Merchant Marines ID.

The ship Emery was assigned to.
Emery's Merchant Marine graduating class.

Posed Merchant Marine photo.
The trailer Evelyn, Joyce, and Audrey were living in
when Emery returned from the Merchant Marines.
Evelyn and Emery starting over after four
years in the Merchant Marines.

Evelyn, Emery, Joyce, Audrey, David, and Stephen.
Joyce and Audrey Hamming it up a bit.

Early family shot. L—R: Audrey, Stephen,
Evelyn, David, Emery, and Joyce.
Easter in front of the House at 2911 South
42nd Street, Kansas City, Kansas.
Easter, 1951, the whole crew.

Another Sunday Best picture. Early
50's probably Easter again.
Labeled: Evelyn must have taken the picture

1956 family photo
Christmas 1956.

David, Kathy, Sarah, Amy, Saylor, Adelaide, and Macklin.

Emery's roughin crew. Cliff Roberts, Jeff Lee, Greg Lee, David Hinkhouse, Emery Hinkhouse/boss man.

Some water under the bridge: L—R: Emery, Stephen, David, Evelyn, Audrey, Joyce.

Emery and brothers, Donald and Virgil Robinson.
Emery's family at his 100th birthday celebration.

Son Stephen and his family: Back row: Adam Hinkhouse,
Greg Koehler, Grant Zimmer, Adam Zimmer, Corrina
Hinkhouse, Henry Koehler, Caroline Koehler, Tara
Hinkhouse Koehler, Easton Zimmer, Hudson Zimmer,
Harrison Koehler, Stephen Hinkhouse, Donna Hinkhouse,
Annabelle Koehler, Heather Hinkhouse Zimmer.

70th wedding anniversary photos.

Chapter 10

Mom Gets Sick

WHEN I GOT home, my mom and dad weren't there. I asked my brothers where they were, and all they could tell me was that they were in Eldorado Springs, Missouri. It was about sixteen or so miles east on Highway 54 from where we lived. Dad had an old Model-A with three flat tires and a dead battery. I pumped up the tires with an old hand pump and borrowed the neighbor's battery charger. The old Ford started right up.

The first thing I did was go to the old country store to buy some food, as there was nothing in the house to eat. The next morning, I searched and found where my mom was. She was being cared for by a doctor who didn't even know what was wrong with her. He was a chiropractor. I called him a quack. I had heard about a doctor in Nevada, Missouri, who had just graduated from the University of Kansas, so I took my mom to see him. He took one look at her and said he thought he knew what was wrong with her but that he would have to run some blood tests to be sure.

Because he could see that my mom was running out of time and was in danger of dying, he said he would put a rush on the tests. He told me to come back in three days and he would know for sure. We went back, and sure enough, he had been right. He said she would have to go into the hospital at once or she might not make it another month. She was in the hospital for about six weeks. When she came home, she could hardly walk, but she started to get better at once.

While she recovered, I worked for a farmer for fifty cents a day for about two or three weeks, and then the government started what was called the Public Works Administration (PWA). But only the head of the family could work, so that left me out. Even though I had been working in my dad's place, as he had to be at the hospital with Mom, the head guy of the PWA didn't approve and told me I had to go home. Fortunately, my step uncle John Wells went to the courthouse, and he must have known someone because he came by and told me I could report for work. I had to walk, but it was only about four-and-half miles. We made forty dollars every two weeks, which was a really good wage for 1935.

My mom's recovery progressed really fast, and she was soon doing all the work that she was used to doing. She was a tough lady. Most people would have given up and died, but she was able to live another fifty-plus years. My brothers had the same illness as my mom and also had to be doctored. It was my job to see that they got their shots twice a week.

November was approaching, and the PWA work on the road was coming to an end. With winter coming, I knew I had to do something so my mom would have money for food and doctor bills. I decided to skip my senior year in high school so I could work and get more money for Mom. The CCC was recruiting another group of boys, so I signed up for the second time. I left in the first part of November 1935.

Chapter 11

Union and Butler CCC Camps

I WAS SENT to Union, Missouri, near St. Louis. I liked the camp and all the boys. The camp had a recreation hall for nights and weekends, and I just loved it. It was like heaven to me ... boxing, volleyball, playing pool. But I didn't like its location. I needed to be closer to home so I could look in on my mom once in a while, as I knew she had her hands full taking my brothers to the doctor twice a week plus all her other duties as an "olden days" farm wife and mother.

I had gotten to be good friends with the top sergeant, so I asked if he thought I could transfer to Butler, Missouri, which was twenty-nine miles from home. He said he hadn't heard of anyone ever doing that but that it wouldn't hurt to try. In about a week, the camp captain called me to his office and I filled out my papers for the transfer.

The papers were sent to Leavenworth, Kansas, and two weeks later, I was on my way to Camp Butler 3755. I didn't know anyone in the barracks I was assigned to, but I had always had an easy time getting acquainted with folks. Elvis Haines had been the one in charge of choosing all the boys who went to the Union Camp, and he had chosen all the boys from his home area. Boy, was he surprised to see me. I learned that he was the one who sent me to Union instead of letting me be closer to home at Butler. So, I thought he was a jerk and had sent me farther away because he was jealous of me that the girls liked me and didn't like him at all. That, of course, was what I thought at the time.

He knew he was in for a hard time, as I later had his job. I never let him forget the evil deed he did to me. We had gone all the way through high school together, but he never liked me because my girlfriend, Ann May was the girl he liked. He always slammed the volleyball down on the littler kids when we played, so no one liked him. He was a good Baptist who later became an alcoholic and died young. Ann May married another guy later, and he was not good to her either.

I arrived at Butler Camp around January 1938 and was there for two six-month terms. While I was there, I joined the National Guard 203 antiaircraft unit. My job at CCC was driving trucks, a 1934 GMC and 1934 international dump truck, which made me assistant leader. That paid an extra six dollars a month. After I gave twenty-five dollars to my mom, my pay was eleven dollars.

While at Butler Camp, I had a good boxing coach and made a little prize money in CCC camp and National Guard boxing, but the only problem was that you had to win or you got nothing. I could always win if I stayed in my weight class or one above, but back then they were allowed to match anyone. I was a good technical boxer and mostly fought defensively, making my opponents tire out by missing me when they punched or jabbed. I usually surprised them because they looked at my slight build and underestimated me. I don't remember being knocked out, but I did see stars a few times. Just the fun of boxing was worth more than the little bit of prize money I earned. I felt good about fighting and soundly whipping two Golden Gloves boxers. I didn't lose many, if any, of the bouts. But I sure got my bell rung pretty soundly more than once.

I worked at different things, including painting or doing anything outside of camp that would make me a little money. One year I took off time from camp and told the top sergeant I would only be gone for two weeks, but I made so much money in northern Iowa picking corn that I stayed six and a half weeks. I made $175, plus I got paid five cents a bushel and picked close to four thousand bushels. Between going to night school and doing outside jobs, along with the National Guard and my boxing time, I had a full schedule.

Another way I made money in the CCC camp was by loaning money to people who were short on cash. I never spent my money on much, so I would loan out a dollar and the borrower would be required to pay back two dollars on the next payday. The first sergeant went along with me on it and would take the two dollars out of their pay to give to me before he gave them what the camp owed them. It turned out to be a pretty good business for me because many of the men were careless with their money and I never had a lack of customers.

In 1936, my brothers had to be treated again for the same sickness Mom had. They were at Mercy Hospital in Kansas City, Missouri, for two months. Going back and forth every week was quite a task for my mom. They would stop by where I was working on the way up, and I would give them whatever money I had from my corn picking to go toward the hospital bill. Mom always cried when she took my money, but it made me feel good to know I was helping the family. Besides, I was getting three meals a day on the farm where I was working.

Chapter 12

The Lost Years, 1937–1940

I BECAME FRIENDS with another camper named Carl Arnold, another good boxer, and we talked a lot about what we were going to do when our time in the CCC was up. We thought we might go to Minnesota. When we decided to try it, he bought a 1934 Chevrolet and soon we were on our way. We both went to work for farmers.

He got paid thirty dollars a month, and I got paid thirty-five dollars. He worked for a Swede, and I worked for a German. Both were good places to work. I worked for the German for two months and then at another farm until I had to go home to help my family move again. The drought and Dust Bowl were still raging in the Great Plains, making for pretty tough times for my folks. I was sure glad I was old enough to help them.

That winter, the winter of 1937, I moved them to a place about six miles north. It was located five miles east of Nevada, Missouri. I stayed home all winter and helped get the place cleaned up and ready for spring work. I wrote Carl a letter and told him I would be coming to Minnesota and asked him to keep his eye open for a job. He was working on a dairy farm where they needed someone really bad. He said I could work there.

I arrived in the early spring. There were thirty cows to milk by hand in addition to grinding the feed and caring for all the livestock. The farmer, Mr. Hawkins, also had 320 acres to farm with four head of spirited wild horses and an Oliver 70 row-type tractor. He didn't know much about wild horses, so I knew I could help him in that department.

I asked Carl how much he was making, and he said thirty-five dollars a month. Considering all the work there was to do and that Mr. Hawkins was crippled and unable to do anything, I held out for forty dollars a month. I worked there until about the first of June. I was getting older and, at least I liked to think, a little wiser. I began to think there must be a better way to make money than by working fourteen hours a day.

I became friends with a man who worked at the Lincoln Hotel, and he said he might get me on staff. I talked to the owner, and he said I could start as a bartender. The job paid forty-five dollars a month plus tips. That sounded better than forty dollars a month for the more than one-hundred-hour weeks I had been putting in on farms.

I hadn't been working at bartending for very long when I realized that wasn't what I wanted for a lifetime career. I got sick and tired of the town riffraff and drunks coming in and throwing their money away while their families were at home struggling to put food on the table. I made friends with a man who traveled all over the country shelling corn, and he offered me $2.50 per hour. With that offer, I gave my notice and quit. I knew I could tend bar at night all I wanted wherever I went. The only place that didn't serve beer in St. James was at the sweet shop where I would later meet my wife.

When I started shelling corn, which was difficult, back-breaking work, it took me about a week to get back into shape. It didn't take long, scooping corn out of the cribs in hot weather.

We were about finished shelling corn when one evening I saw a bunch of trucks with W.E. Wiley Electric Co. written on the sides. I asked what they were going to do, and the man said they were starting to build electric lines because of Roosevelt's Rural Electrification Act (REA) and that they would be hiring in about a week. That sounded perfect for me because Mr. Smith wasn't going to need me much longer. This was another time when one of Franklin Roosevelt's New Deal programs gave my life a real boost.

In 1937, I was hired by the REA and went to work digging holes, which were five to six feet deep, for the electrical poles. I did that the first day, and when night came, I asked the head boss, who was superintendent over the whole operation, if there was anything else I could do. He asked me where I was from, and I told him I was from southern Missouri on the border of the Ozarks. He asked if I was good with an ax, and I said anything would beat digging holes. He said I could trim trees, and I sure liked that idea. I liked climbing those tall Cottonwoods, and I learned to climb with climbing spikes, which would later help me climb poles for another job.

I worked for the REA until sometime in January 1938, I think, when they shut the operation down until the spring. I hadn't been home for about nine months, so I went home and helped Dad cut a large wood pile to be buzzed up by a man who did that every winter. It was easier than doing it by hand and faster, too.

I was talking to a man in town one day about a job, and he asked if I was drawing Social Security. I didn't even know what he was talking about. That was the first job that I needed a Social Security card and number to work. Social Security was new to everyone. I went to the Social Security office and signed up, never thinking anyone could get money and not work for it. About two weeks later, I was surprised when I went to the mailbox and there was a check for thirteen dollars. That meant I could make fifty-two dollars a month, which was more than I'd ever made working. It came in real handy, as my folks were moving again, about half a mile away—the shortest move we had ever made.

This was yet another Roosevelt program that helped destitute, struggling people like us, though with the work I had been doing, we had at least been able to pay bills. Sometimes in life, a man just needs a few bucks to get him through to the next day and back on his feet. Roosevelt provided that kind of help to people who needed money now and not later, money they did not have to feel humiliated to accept. I bought Dad some hay and feed and some seed corn for spring planting.

Things were looking up. My mom and little brothers were feeling good, and the boys would soon be on their way to having good jobs of their own. Now that I'd gotten the folks moved to a better place (the Fleshman Place) and everyone was in better health, I could go back to Minnesota. It was a great relief not having so much to worry about and feeling like I could get on with my own life.

I don't want to give the impression that everything was always bad. I always had a girlfriend. My high school girlfriend ran off with an older guy from Tulsa, Oklahoma. I still see her every year at high school reunions. I had one girlfriend, Mary, who was killed when a train hit her car. She had also been going with another guy during my travels and jobs. I had just about given up on having a steady girlfriend. Her sister Violet liked me and even sent me letters, but somehow we just didn't click, if you know what I mean.

I attended my national guard meetings every four weeks, which paid a dollar monthly. I had a few boxing matches at the armory. There were always a lot of people there because the matches were the biggest thing going on in town. I made a little money boxing. Skunks and possums were still bringing $1.50 to $2.50 apiece, but there weren't many to catch and trap. The drought had taken its toll on my fur trapping business, too.

I repaired the Model A for Dad by having a new windshield put in and installing better tires. And since Dad never changed the oil or greased a car, I had that done along, with adding new points and plugs. I did everything except the windshield, so it didn't cost much. The windshield cost more than the rest of the repairs put together.

I drew my Social Security checks for about four months and then headed back to Minnesota. I always felt guilty, getting money without working for it. I got to Minnesota a little before the REA started up again, so I tended bar at night and worked for the superintendent of the REA corps during the day. I jumped at that chance because it meant I would be in one place all the time and wouldn't have to go farther east with the construction company, building the lines.

I had a room with a man I worked with on the REA, but I had to eat my meals out or buy things to eat in my room. I ate a lot of sandwiches and soup, whatever I could buy cheap; you can't buy much when you don't make much.

Chapter 13

How I Met My Wife-To-Be

IN THE SUMMER of 1940, I was hanging out in the evenings at the Lincoln Hotel and Bar, where I used to work (and still did some nights). One night I decided to go up the street to a place called the Sweet Shop, where the high school girls hung out. They couldn't go to bars because they weren't old enough, and they liked us older guys. The Sweet Shop was about the only place in town where they didn't sell beer.

When I got there, there was no other customer except the resident cat and me. I was holding the cat when in walked a couple I knew with someone I had never seen (Evelyn), and I had thought I knew everyone in town. They were going someplace, and I asked if I could hitch a ride and go along. They agreed.

Not knowing about this newfound girl, I didn't even asked her for a date. I didn't figure she would go anyway until she found out more about me. Back in our time, girls could be a little choosey because there were about three boys for every girl in the town of St. James. There were boys in town from about every state in the Midwest because this was a rich farming country that had never experienced a crop failure or drought so far north. The farmers also liked to take advantage of the cheap help that the misery of the Great Depression had caused. But there was work for wages to be had in Minnesota.

I heard from someone that the girl I had met in the Sweet Shop was going to be at the Fourth of July celebration in Lake Okoboji, Iowa, a town about seventy miles from St. James. Since I didn't have a car, I talked a friend of mine into going. I never did let him know why I really wanted to go. We had been there for about a half hour when we ran into—guess who—Evelyn and her brother Alvin, his girlfriend, and another girl called Ellen Michaelson, who was with a guy named Merle Miller.

Well, needless to say, I was immediately smitten. The only way I know how to say it is, "When you're struck, you're struck." She was the most beautiful woman I had ever seen, and she was friendly and had a very shy smile that I really liked. She would put her chin to her chest, tilt her head, and look at me with a twinkle in her eye. I was a goner.

After a little chitchat, I asked if she would like to ride on the roller-coaster. We rode it twice. While we were walking around, I finally got up the courage to ask her to ride home with me and my friend. She said she would have to ask her brother. We found him, and he said, "No, you better not." He was being the typical big brother, so I asked, "Do you have a reason why she should not go with me?" He replied that he did not, so I took her by the hand, and she went with me for the rest of the day, doing what all young people do. My friend did not find a girl for himself that day.

We got home around midnight, and we made a date for the following week. We were together from then on and still are. At the time, I thought what a good wife she would make for someone, not thinking it would really come true.

Emery Carl Hinkhouse, Jr.

In 1939 and 1940, before I met Evelyn in St. James, I had been working for Co-Op Electric all year, climbing poles and whatever else there was to do, taking care of about six or seven hundred miles of line. Back then we didn't have all the modern equipment they have today.

When Evelyn and I had been going together for about six months, we decided we would like to be together permanently. We were both alone and had no place of our own. It took some thinking on our part to figure out how we were going to afford marriage, but it was the kind of thinking that gave me hope and a real look at a bright future with this beautiful, nice woman with a shy smile and a twinkle in her eye.

Chapter 14

Starting from Scratch

IT WAS THE summer of 1940, and I came to work one morning and found out that I was going to be transferred to Jeffers, Minnesota, about sixty miles west of St. James. I wasn't happy about it and neither was Evelyn because that meant we would only see each other on weekends. I also didn't like the man I had to work with. He was the type to lord his authority over his workers, me in particular, it seemed. He was the head lineman, and that meant I got all the bad jobs like going out in the middle of the night to get the electricity back on so farmers could milk their cows. It could be dangerous work, especially when it was dark, raining, or snowing. Years later, after I had left that job, I found out that he wound up getting electrocuted on one of his calls.

I was staying with the aforementioned head lineman and his wife, paying room and board, when Evelyn's brother Tony and I decided to get a place together. I had gotten Tony a job helping build new electric lines for Co-Op Electric, too.

To make a long story short, I got tired of running back to St. James every weekend to be with my future wife, so we decided to get married. We tied the knot on January 8, 1941 in Jeffers, Minnesota, in a Lutheran church. I paid the pastor five dollars and spent twelve dollars on a wedding ring. Evelyn paid ten dollars for her wedding dress. We waited until after Evelyn's birthday on January 4 so she would be nineteen years old. As I mentioned before, when you're struck you're struck.

Two weeks after our wedding, I lost my job at Co-Op Electric. I think my boss was mad about losing the rent I had been paying him. I believe Harlin Guernsey, the boss, partnered up with this guy in the electric shop in Jeffries and together they "double dipped", which means they made their wages from the REA and charged farmers extra for hooking them up to the electricity, a pretty lucrative side business at the expense of the REA. They figured they could make money as employees of Co-Op Electric *and* ask farmers if they could run the lines from the road to their houses for an extra charge to the farmers, who were eager to get electricity. I don't think it was entirely legit, but they did it anyway, and I lost my job in the process. I never told on them, though.

It was the middle of winter and the Depression was still going on. There were no jobs in Minnesota except for working on a farm, if you could even find that. It was a back-against-the-wall start to a new life: I had a new bride and no job. I owned a 1936 Ford that I let go back to where I bought it, and we stayed with Evelyn's brother Larry and his wife, Iris, until spring and warmer weather. I found a job for thirty-five dollars a month on a farm located in Hanska, Minnesota. It was four-and-a-half miles west, and because I no longer had a car, I had to walk morning and night, sometimes in twenty-degree temperatures or colder. When spring came I had saved enough money to buy a 1929 Model A coup for twenty-five dollars, and boy did it turn out to be a good car. I still have a picture of that truck.

We moved to St. James and rented an upstairs place from a good friend of mine for twenty dollars a month. It was a plain room with a dresser and a wash basin and a shared bathroom down the hall. I knew a contractor who was remodeling a funeral home across the street, and he gave me a job digging out the dirt under the building to make a basement under his house. The only equipment we had was a Model T dump truck, a dirt scrapper, and an old pick and shovel. I also did six or seven hours of work each night, plowing and working for farmers; some of the late model tractors had lights.

I also tended bar some weekends at the Lincoln Hotel Bar. It was considered "swanky" by the standards back then. Soon my work at the funeral home was about done, so because I had worked for Roberts Bros. Trucking one season hauling peas from Spring Valley, Minnesota, to Rochester Cannery, I thought I would try that. The bad part about that was I would have to be gone for six weeks in June and July. I got two of Evelyn's brothers, Tony and Bud, jobs there, too, because it was better to have someone you knew with you. Bud was only fifteen years old at the time. We hauled peas for about six weeks and then went back and hauled sweet corn—all for thirty-five cents an hour.

That is where Evelyn's brother Tony met his wife-to-be, Harriet. She worked and cooked where we ate and slept in bunk shacks and the dining shack.

After hauling corn from Spring Valley to Rochester, my work across Minnesota was through. I was glad to get back to St. James and look for other work so I could be at home and around my new wife for good. I went to work for someone closer to home, whom I had worked for before, this time digging ditches and laying tile for the city at thirty cents per hour. I dug ditches by hand, no machines. I learned how to be a crummer, which meant clearing up the ditch with a long-handled shovel behind the main guy who worked the spade, carving our way through the earth like moles.

Chapter 15

In Business for Myself

I HADN'T WORKED at ditching for very long before I realized there must be a better, and hopefully, easier way to earn money. I heard that the government was starting to buy all the flax straw they could get their hands on. They used flax straw to make the linen needed in the lines attached to parachutes. Everyone with a truck started hauling flax straw, so I got a job helping load trucks with a pitch fork, which I soon found, was worse than ditching.

I had been working that job for about a week when I found out the men with trucks were getting four dollars per ton for hauling, so I started looking for a truck. Since everyone had already bought their trucks, they were hard to find because WWII had just started, and the government had taken over the auto factories to make military equipment.

I was in my second week of loading Mr. Miller's truck for forty cents an hour while he made four dollars a ton when I heard about a Model A truck in storage at the Ford garage. It had been used for hauling freight at the depot and was in perfect condition, but it was missing one of the dual wheels on the back. The man said he had wanted a hundred dollars for it but now just wanted to get it out of the way and would take fifty dollars. I offered him twenty-five dollars down and twenty-five dollars in a month, but he told me to forget about the other twenty-five, so I bought a three-legged truck for twenty-five dollars and made more than $200 in the first week. It pays to make good friends, and I think back on my experience picking coal when I was younger and buying that wagon to haul coal in with my profits. The right tools are crucial to make more money than just a laborer's wage. And the right tool pays for itself over and over again. Here is yet another example of a person who helped me find my way to the better life I so much wanted and sought.

The second week of hauling, I bought a tire and wheel and made the bed longer and built another flat section over the cab so I could haul bigger loads. My wife's brother Tony knew how to remodel trucks and helped me do it. He was also hauling, but with an REO Speed Wagon truck, and his brother Bud had gotten a truck, so we decided to get a tractor and a loader to make things faster and the work less backbreaking. It all worked out pretty well, only Bud and Tony would not work early in the morning at sunrise and wanted to quit before dark. I went to work in the dark and came home in the dark. Dawn to Dusk was always my motto to get ahead in life. I never had so much money in my life thanks to that old Model A Ford, not to mention what I had learned in my life up to that point about the virtues of hard work.

I was a proud papa when our first daughter, Joyce, was born. Back then, the doctor came to the house for deliveries. I was the one who named all our kids, and I named her after a girl I knew in grade school because I had always liked that name. I wanted to get out of that one-room house so we could have more room because we now had a child. I heard about a farm for rent in Nevada, Missouri, that sounded like a good place, so we prepared to move.

I bought a four-wheel trailer, loaded the few personal items we had onto it, hooked it to the Model A, and moved to Missouri with Evelyn, little Joyce, and Alice, Evelyn's sister. Alice had no other place to live because her mom and dad, Ole and Marie, had separated and Marie had moved back to St. James, Minnesota, to take a job as a housekeeper to support herself. She would not have been able to afford to take care of Alice, so Alice ended up living with us. We stopped for a few things we needed to set up housekeeping, and once they were settled, I went back to Minnesota to finish hauling flax, which lasted for about six more weeks. Then I drove the Model A four hundred miles back home to Missouri.

Most farmers were still farming with horses, so I bought four head. One pair and a wagon cost a hundred dollars and a second team of horses cost me eighty dollars. At the local hardware store, I purchased whatever else it would take to begin to run a farm. I bought a mule to slaughter for pig feed, which was a practice some used at that time, but my brother, Virgil, who lived next door to us and road the mule all the way home from the sale, grew attached to the mule and liked him, so he wouldn't let me butcher the mule and it turned out to be a blessing in disguise. That mule became a "working Jesse," as we called it back then. He was a really good work animal and dependable pulling the plow and harrow. We farmed sixty acres of corn and twenty acres of oats. We lived close by my folks, so I was able to use some of my dad's farm equipment to work the land, and that mule helped pull a lot of that equipment.

We had been moved for about one month when I realized I would need some way to make a little money because I knew the small amount I had saved from hauling flax would be needed for essentials necessary to start a new life farming, so I got a job working for the Missouri Pacific Railroad. I worked ten-hour night shifts, from 8:00 p.m. to 6:00 a.m., seven nights a week. They called it the dead man's shift, but they were a good group of men to work with. It was 1942, and I was twenty-five years old. I ran our farm in the daytime. Sleep was a word I would not be closely acquainted with during that stretch of time.

On credit, I bought my mom and dad seven cows and four more for myself and started selling milk to the cheese factory. With the salary from the railroad, and now the money from selling milk and eggs, we were doing pretty well. My wife was a good help-mate and helped milk the cows and take care of the laying hens. One memory I have was that we had 207 chicks in a building that caught on fire, and she saved them all by carrying them upstairs into the house in her apron.

It was a tough go. I could not have planted as much corn and milo if not for my younger brothers, Donald and Virgil. They were so good to help in the fields. I made some extra money buying old farm machinery at the sale barn, bringing it home, repairing and painting it, and taking it back for resale. I looked for bargains. I would buy anything cheap like harnesses, saddles, and any kind of animals like horses, mules, calves, or pigs. I never intended to keep them for more than two or three weeks. I didn't get rich, but I had a lot of fun "horse trading," and I used the money to buy more young cattle so I could increase my dairy herd. I had just gotten everything going pretty well when my folks bought the farm I was farming on, which meant I would lose the land I was farming. They bought the eighty acres that was tillable. The eighty acres that I was living on was mostly wooded and untillable. So, while I was happy to see my folks pick up a pretty good piece of property, I still had to find another way to make money. So, there I was again, in a tight spot.

Audrey, our second child, was born November 24 of that year, 1942, in our little house in Nevada, Missouri, with the help of a country doctor. WW II cranked into full gear and all the young men around me were joining the armed services. So now I had two little ones who needed food, shelter, and a chance in life, and I was responsible for making sure they got that. I was sure proud to see Audrey arrive and happy to have a lifelong friend for Joyce. I moved to Kansas City, Kansas in 1943, bought a little trailer to live in, and got a job at the Cudday Hays Packing Plant. I worked in the smoke house to start, and then, because of my Natioal Guard and CCC experience, they moved me to guard duty. The wages were about 80-90 cents an hour. No one was going to get rich on those wages, so I started thinking more and more about joining the military.

Chapter 16

The Merchant Marines

ONE NIGHT IN 1944, Vice President Truman came on the radio, begging for men to serve. He promised young men like me all the benefits the armed forces would receive after the war if we joined the US Merchant Marines. Since the farms were not available to me to be a tenant farmer at this time, and I also realized the job at the packing plant was a dead-end street, I decided to join. I held a sale and sold everything we had except our 1935 Chevrolet, even my old Model A truck that had been responsible for everything we had earned. It brought $125 (a $100 profit). My sale netted about $8,000. I bought $6,000 in war bonds and a brand-new Red Arrow house trailer for Evelyn, Joyce, and Audrey to live in and left to join the US Merchant Marines.

That was the end of the National Guard and farming for me for a while. Because I am legally blind in one eye, I had to fake the eye test to pass the physical exam for the merchant marines. I did my good eye first and switched the hand holding the card to make it look like I had changed eyes. They must not have been paying too close of attention.

I would be leaving four girls behind—my wife, my daughters, and also my wife's sister, Alice, who stayed with Evelyn so she could help care for Joyce and Audrey while Evelyn worked nights at a restaurant next door to the trailer. (None of this worked out, as I will explain later.)

I had parked the trailer on Minnesota Ave. in Kansas City, Kansas. Next door was the restaurant where Evelyn's sister Alice met her first husband, Jim Houchin, which began a very long, trying episode in her life. He was the cook at the restaurant. She found out later that he was a polygamist and had wives in other states whom he had left behind. He also eventually left her on her own with three kids to fend for herself, but that's another story for another place and time.

Wives like Evelyn, who were left behind because of the war, did not have an easy time of it, especially when a sister who needed almost as much watching as the girls was thrown into the mix. Evelyn had a hard time of things during my four-year absence. She took on the role of a single mom, as many wives did during those trying times. I would have liked to have left her in better circumstances, but times were rough, and I thought the military would solve my financial problems.

I was about to embark on my first big mistake in life, serving in the US Merchant Marines. All the things Truman promised us after the war ended turned out to be false, just a lot of hot air to get economically depressed young men to join. We merchant seamen never received any of the benefits that were promised to us by Truman's GI Bill, which was one of the reasons I joined, because of the security of a steady income it offered.

I was sent to Sheepshead Bay on Long Island, New York, a suburb of New York City, for boot camp in late February 1944. Since I had been in the National Guard and CCC camp and was older than a lot of recruits, I had a good resume and was given a temporary rating as leader over forty-eight Georgia Tech and Alabama State college students who were a bunch of real good kids. It was tough on them because most of them had never had a job and were really soft. For me, it was like being on vacation because I was used to sixteen-hour work days and the military work day was much shorter than that.

My wife came to see me one weekend while I was in boot camp, and after graduation, I was sent to Seattle in late April and early May. I didn't see her for a long time after that. In Seattle, I was assigned to the steamship, *Columbia* and made two trips to Alaska before I ended up on the Steamship, Joseph J. Kinyoun and traveled the dangerous waters of the Pacific war zone. When I went home on my first and only leave in the four years I was in the military, I saw that things were a little out of hand at home and recognized that Evelyn needed to move nearer to her mother, so I immediately moved her back to Minnesota so she would be near her folks and my girls would be in a better environment. I did not want them growing up in the city around, what I considered to be, low-life people hanging around in the streets at all hours. In addition, my sister-in-law Alice, as I previously mentioned, had decided to marry and have a baby with Jim Houchin, so my wife was left alone. I did not feel at all good about that and felt they all needed to be closer to family.

I then returned to Seattle with no small amount of concern in my mind for my wife and two daughters, who I would be leaving behind for the next two and a half years. I guess I thought serving duty in the war zone might take my mind off things, so with my friend Bob Buchler, because the government was paying double for duty in the war zone, I volunteered for the South Pacific war zone, which turned out to be a very dangerous, taxing, and long journey in my life. Not to mention, being in a war zone did *not* alleviate my worries about Evelyn and the girls. Their safety and well-being were a constant worry, and homesickness weighed heavily on my shoulders.

It took us two weeks to sail to the little island of Enewetale and another week to arrive in Manila in the Philippines because we were on a zigzag course to make it more difficult for the Japanese to track our routes. It was not a perfect system, but it did make it more difficult for them to find us. If all our ships were on a zigzag path, the Japanese couldn't attack an entire group of ships; they could only attack one at a time, which made their attacks much more difficult and wasteful to conduct. After a while, I got used to all the war noise and blackouts, settled into my daily routine, and waited for the war to end. My biggest problem was constant worry for my wife and little girls.

We went from the Philippines to Okinawa. (Bud, my wife's brother, was in Okinawa at the same time I was, though neither of us knew it.) Then we went to Saipan and Tinian and around the circle back to the Philippines, dodging torpedoes and suicide planes along the merchant path. I don't think the Japanese saw as much of a need to waste much time on an old liberty ship like ours; they were after the big aircraft carriers, troop ships, and tankers.

My duties on ship were easy compared to what I had been used to all my life. I would do my shift and double for someone who wanted to go ashore or get some time off. Usually I could make ten or twelve dollars extra. All the extra cash I made, along with my poker money, I sent home to Evelyn. I was a pretty good poker player.

We went from Okinawa back to Saipan and Tinian and from there back to the Philippines and were docked there for seven and a half months, mostly at bay, just sitting. We finally went back to Okinawa and were there, convoying to go to

Japan, when the first atomic bomb was dropped. We didn't hear about it until days later. When we did hear, we just couldn't believe it until we got back to Manila in the Philippines. We tied up at pier 13, and it was there that we heard the war had ended on August 14, 1945, Joyce's birthday. What a great way to celebrate a birthday.

We unloaded our cargo and thought we would embark for home, but much to our surprise, we were sent to Thailand after a cargo of rice for the city of Manila. We did that for thirteen months and then finally loaded the ship with copra (the insides of coconuts) and sailed for the US. We docked and went ashore in San Francisco sometime in September 1946.

Those thirteen months seemed longer than the time we spent during the war, not knowing when we would be going home. We were paid but couldn't get discharged until we took all our medical exams for South Pacific diseases and whatever else they were looking for. My buddy Robert Buckler had gone through boot camp with me and from boot camp until that last trip back home to Kansas City. In later years, despite the fact that we had lived on the ocean for all that time, he drowned in the Wyandotte County Lake in Kansas City, Kansas.

After all the time I spent in South Pacific, I was never sick one day after that with anything. Some of the crew contacted malaria, which caused jaundice. Others who were not careful about keeping their boots and feet dry suffered jungle rot, which was a nasty rash that caused their feet to become infected, sore, and swollen. One of the main problems as the war had drug on was finding good food. All our coolers had broken down and our meat and vegetables spoiled, so we ate pretty poorly until we got back to Philippines. Our first cook really knew a lot of ways to fix rice. (We were loaded with plenty of it—more than

13,000 tons.) He could even use spoiled eggs and make them taste good with cinnamon and whatever else he mixed in.

One other event worth mentioning is how we went through the worst typhoon ever recorded before or since in the Pacific, the Okinawa Typhoon of 1945. It happened two weeks after the war ended. It lasted four days and nights and we had ground swells for days afterward. The military lost 80 percent of all the ships that were marooned in Buckner Bay and at Yellow Beach. Our captain took us out to sea, killed all machinery in the engine room, dropped the fore and aft anchors, and we rode out the storm. We never lost a man, but we had to tie ourselves into our beds if we went to bunk. I remember that a lot of the men, including me, promised God they would go to church if they made it through the storm. I kept that promise, as will be seen later in my story.

After my arrival home, in September of 1946 something told me to call home before I left for St. James, Minnesota, where Evelyn had been living the last time we wrote to each other. I found out that my wife and girls had moved to Walker, Missouri. Evelyn told me she moved to get away from her feuding parents. When I arrived home, my girls didn't even know me, but it didn't take long for me to win them over. Evelyn had pretty much no money left because the move had cost her all our savings. So when I got home, we were back at square one, financially speaking.

I had left the States weighing 155 pounds and came home weighing 130, but I was really healthy and ready to go to work. It had taken about all my farm sale money, along with the allotment and money I sent home, for Evelyn and the girls to live on, so I was back where I had started when I had my farm sale, only without that money. The whole time I was in the USMM, I had only drawn one hundred dollars of my pay, so with what I sent home and the money I had put aside when my term of service came to an end, I had saved $6,000, which meant I had a better start looking for work because I had a little cushion of money to give me time to be choosey about the job I took.

Because we came back thirteen months after everyone else, all the good jobs had been taken and there were no farms to rent. Things looked pretty bad, so I headed back to Minnesota with Evelyn and the kids to see what I could find. It was the start of flax straw hauling season, so I bought a 1933 Ford truck and a house trailer and went to work. I hauled flax straw until the middle of January. Then we moved to Kansas City and I began job hunting.

I went to work at Gustin-Bacon (an insulation plant) for seventy-five and half cents an hour. I was hired as an electrician's helper. The job turned out to be no good because the title meant that I was the person who blew the insulation out of the electric motors with a blower. I was lucky not to have kept that job, considering the lung problems later suffered by the people who were forced to work there for much longer periods of time.

Five-and-a-half months later, my brother Virgil and I went to work for the Union Pacific Railroad for eighty-seven-and-a-half cents an hour. It would have been a better job if not for one man who thought he was the boss. The actual boss was a really nice man. After three years in the water service with UP, I transferred over into round house as an electrician's helper on diesel locomotives. In the late 1940s and early 1950s, they were switching from steam to diesel.

I bought our first house at 2023 North 16th Street in Kansas City, Kansas, in the summer of 1947. We thought we had a mansion after living in the little trailer house. The house cost

$3,750. I put $2,500 down. That was the first time I had ever made a payment on anything.

My two boys, David and Stephen, were born in that house. It was a large house with an detached garage. I rented out two of the upstairs rooms and my old trailer and made the garage into a rental apartment. My brother Virgil and his wife, Coleen, rented the garage from us. With the rent money coming in and me working two jobs, we were making a go of it.

I got my brother Donald a job at the railroad with the survey gang. It was a better job than I had, but I thought it was nice that three brothers could be working at the same place.

We lived at 2023 N 16th Street for five and half years. I sold it for $5,000 and bought a little house on Strawberry Hill in Kansas City, which I sold for $2,000 even before the closing of the house we were living in on 16th Street was complete. In all, my profit for the five and a half years was $4,300.

My brother Donald and two of his high school friends had a room in that house and Alice, Evelyn's sister, had lived upstairs. We left a lot of memories at that place but thought it was time to move because the neighborhood was changing fast. I wanted to get closer to Johnson County and better schools. We left behind many friends that we had made in that five-and-half- years because it was there that we started going to church and trying to turn our spiritual life around. That made quite a difference in my lifestyle. That was where and when I quit drinking beer and smoking cigarettes. I had only smoked for a short time, but it was still pretty hard to quit. It was 1947, and I have never wanted a cigarette since.

Chapter 17

Postwar Life in the Suburbs

OUR SECOND HOUSE was located at 2911 South 42nd Street in Kansas City, Kansas. We moved there in 1951. I had heard about a small house on two and a half acres near the Johnson County line. The old couple who owned it lived in Lenexa, Kansas. When we went out to talk to them, it seemed like we traveled a hundred miles along nothing but an old winding road. We had never been in this area before, but we finally arrived in the dark and they were there to greet us. They were really nice to talk to, and they priced the house and one-and-quarter-acre for $5,000, and they wanted an extra $1,000 for the other one and a quarter acre. I told them I could only afford the $5,000. They went into another room and talked it over and said we could have the complete two and a half acres for $5,500. Reluctantly, we agreed to their offer. Later, in 1954, we built our first new house on the added one-and-a-quarter-acre strip of land we got for that extra $500. So it ended up being a good deal.

That small house at 2911 was too cramped for a family of four and had only one bedroom, so I built a large bedroom on the north end of the house and hand dug the dirt out of the basement with a spade, a long-handled shovel, and a wheelbarrow. Joyce and Audrey helped pull the wheelbarrow up the steps on a board plank, and I hauled the dirt about three hundred feet behind the house and dumped it to fill in a ditch. The boys were too little to help but had fun playing in the dirt and watching the basement being dug. The four of them shared the single bedroom and Evelyn and I took over the new addition. Later, I added a third bedroom on the back of the house so the girls could have their own bedroom, as they were becoming teenagers and needed more privacy.

A lot of history in our lives was created at this 2911 address. It was where I was able to get a better job at Fairbanks Morse as an electrician. I worked there for the next twenty-one years. Nearby, we also built our first church, an Assembly of God church pastored by Brother Gary Golf. We called each other brother and sister in the Assembly of God churches. Our family grew close to the Golf family and socialized with them because they had a similarly aged boy who our boys liked to play with. As time passed, the building itself hosted many different pastors who came and went and moved on quite frequently to other callings. The building still stands today. It served as a church for a long time and is now a daycare center for children.

It was at 2911 that our boys, David and Stephen, started school at Junction Grade School and where they had plenty of room to romp and play and numerous good neighborhood boys to chum with. The girls, Joyce and Audrey, were old enough to work in the garden I planted every year, but sometimes they couldn't tell the weeds from the real plants. The smart weed and pepper plant looked similar, and one time they pulled all the pepper plants by mistake and left all the weeds. Evelyn canned a lot of vegetables out of that garden.

The kids had a pet donkey, two goats, a dog, and just about every other kind of farm animal you can name over the years we were there. They all learned the value of work because their daily duties included taking care of those animals. It was a great place for the kids to grow up. It sure beat living in town.

As time passed and we vistited our old neighborhood we saw a neighborhood that had given way to crime and dilapidation. In 2017, I traveled back to that old address at 2023 with my two sons and found a police officer looking for bullet shells from a drive-by shooting that had happened the night before. Our old house was gone and all that grew in the yard was weeds and trash.

Circling back to my job at Fairbanks-Morse, it only took me five minutes to get hired. I went out into the plant area and looked for the plant engineer. He had a Swedish name—Gustafson. I told him my wife was Swedish, and he told me I could start work the next morning, but because it was Thursday, I told him I needed to give the railroad at least a four-day notice. This was another time that Evelyn, my wife, became a very important instrument of positive change. Who would have thought that her heritage would one day land me a job that became the springboard to a better and brighter future?

I reported for work at Fairbanks Morse on Monday, August 14, 1952 at 8 o'clock in the morning. I had to go through personnel. The man in personnel didn't know about my conversation with the Swede and said he did the hiring and that I was not needed at this time. He wanted to be the big shot. It was really a letdown, as I had already quit my other job and was suddenly unemployed. So I went around to the west gate one more time and told the guard I had an appointment with the plant engineer. He called him on the loud speaker, and the engineer came right out. He was real put out when he heard my story. He took me to personnel himself and told the guy to never turn away anyone he sent in again. I had created my first enemy, at least at this place of employment, but I later lived to see him fired.

I had taken on a big job, as all my electrical knowledge had been outside on high line work and diesel locomotives. I was fortunate that the construction men were still hooking up and putting machines into operation. I had time to ask a lot of questions before they left. I also sent off for a *National Electrical Code* book and did some boning up. I was lucky to have the experience from Roosevelt's REA (Rural Electrification Administration) under my belt. Thank you again, President Roosevelt.

Chapter 18

The First Church, Loaves and Fish, a Labor of Love

WE ATTENDED OUR old church for a while after we moved to 2911 but decided we needed to find a church in our own neighborhood. There was a four-and-a-half acre piece of land with a two-bedroom house for sale down the street from us, close to Shawnee Drive. It was listed for $5,000. The preacher who would become pastor of the church I would help build on that acreage, Reverend David Golf, was holding a two week revival in town. In case you don't know what a revival is, it is an intense window of time when guest preachers try to fire up the congregation to be better stewards of their Christian faith, and also to gain new converts. He was the minister at our old church in the city. He said he would help us get the church going. When we closed the deal on the property, he moved into the house until the church was built.

I went to Argentine Building and Loan and borrowed the money for a down payment with Rev. David Goff. He signed papers with me for the land. So we had land but no church yet. I went to work digging the ditches needed for the footers by hand. I also mixed the cement myself, by hand, and poured the footers for the building structure. Alan Hartford, one of my church friends, helped me with the work. He was a willing and good worker and had some knowledge of carpentry. I think the Lord sent him along at just the right time. I had gotten him a job where I worked, and he returned the favor by helping me on this project.

I worked nights on the project because I had a day job at Fairbanks and Morse. The preacher didn't help with the manual labor, as he was not one for that type of work. We were thankful to have him as a minister, though. The $860 building fund was running out when Rev. Goff's dad offered to loan us $5,000 more to finish the project. He recognized that we really meant business because of all the hard work we had already done. He owned a ranch that grew mostly wheat in western Kansas and one on which they eventually struck oil.

We had quite the struggle with building the project. We had just gotten the footers and foundation completed when a petition was started around the neighborhood to keep us from continuing. The Catholics in the neighborhood refused to sign it, even though we were a Protestant church and, on top of that, a rambunctious and noisy Assembly of God church, which had services that could be distinctly heard outside the church's walls, especially in the summer. So, fortunately, the petition died practically before it started.

The biggest problem I had was getting good help and a carpenter who knew carpentry. I didn't know that trade at that point in my life. The first carpenter we employed didn't get along with the pastor, so he quit quickly. Luckily, my brother-in-law Earl Nelson had just moved back to Kansas City from California and was an excellent carpenter. It was good timing that might have involved the Lord. I traded him a free place to stay if he would help me on the church. As people could see, there was going to be a church despite all our setbacks, so we started getting more help from people who respected what we were trying to accomplish.

One man offered us an electric circular saw. I don't remember his name, but he was from the neighborhood. Power tools were a new idea at that time, so we were afraid to use it. He gave us some quick lessons, and that changed the speed of the project quite a bit and made the cutting a lot easier. We entered the age of power tools on that project. That was one of the best things that happened. He was a gentleman who did not attend church. You never know where your help will come from, but I did know who sent him along.

Finally, after working a lot of nights and weekends and with the aid of some volunteer help, we finished the church at the end of February of 1953 and had our first service. One man who had helped us for many hours, Gilbert Harrison, became a regular member of our new church, but tragically, he was killed a short time later when a drunk driver, driving the wrong way, hit him head on in the days of no seat belts. At least he did a little work for the Lord before he departed and remains a strong memory when I reflect on this great adventure.

Eight people attended our first service, but by Easter Sunday we had progressed to an attendance of one hundred. That old church has provided an abundance of great memories. My wife had the most to do of anyone, cooking for all the help who had worked on the church and working up front as song leader and young people's leader. I served as Sunday school superintendent, and as time passed and the membership grew, other eager people came along to fill important positions within the church. New and old Christians were very willing to become part of God's new adventure for all of us. As we called it back then, they felt they had "the calling" to do God's work.

To conclude this part of my story, the old church is still there and serves as a reminder to me and others that determination and "elbow grease" is sometimes more effective when chasing dreams than brains, and no ambitions or shouted hallelujahs and amens can ever match that. I sought sanctity in working with my hands and accomplishing tasks.

To this day, that church is the mother church for many other churches built in our city by other ambitious young Christians who wanted to go off on their own and start churches in other parts of the city. I later became the leader of the construction of several different church projects. I guess you might say that I felt this was my calling, since I wasn't one who liked to speak so much and shout hallelujah as the teachers and preachers were able to do.

Chapter 19

The Beginnings of My Homebuilding Career

ALL THE EXPERIENCE I had gathered while building the church got me thinking that maybe I could make a living at that sort of thing, as one thing often leads to another in life. I formed a partnership with my brother-in-law Earl Nelson, and we took on remodeling and repair work, which led to Earl deciding to build a new house for himself and his family. It was my first house and would lead to a long career of building more than one thousand houses in the Kansas City area and beyond. When we finished Earl's house, I decided that since I was learning this new trade of house building, I would build one for myself and my family like he did.

Sweet Lumber Company, located on Merriam Lane and Roe Boulevard in Kansas City, had started a precut home building business to attract more customers to their lumber products. I bought the third home that came off their line, and that became the little three-bedroom house we built on the extra one-and-a-half-acre plot at the 2911 S. 42nd Street address. The same Gilbert Harrison who had helped with the church helped me every evening and on weekends. It was one of his last chances to help before the auto accident.

Sweet Lumber must have been impressed with how I built my house because their superintendent, Gene Smith, called me into his office and asked me if I would be interested in building their homes on a permanent basis for other customers. I turned down the offer at first, but after I went home and thought about it, I decided that if he asked again, I would accept the offer. He called about three days later with the same offer and so began my long and prosperous career building Standard Homes, as they were called. My career was at the leading edge of a big building boom across the nation that lasted for at least the next twenty years.

All the work we had done on the church and the knowledge we had picked up remodeling and building our own houses ended up leading to this new adventure, but as we were to learn, it would be a lot different building houses for other people.

Building that first house for my family was a good experience. I had to get a loan, and having a credit background because of the church helped me get one for $10,000. The fact that I had already obtained the one and a quarter acres to build the house on was certainly a great boost to get me started.

My kids were growing up fast. The boys were old enough to help on the construction job. They could hand us nails and serve as all-around helpers. I knew they would be in high school soon, and I felt the need to make more money to help pay their way through. As it turns out, I was right about high school being more expensive than first through eighth grades, and later when they chose to go to college at Kansas University, the real expense hit.

The trip to Lenexa to bargain for the property at 2911, as the Lord provides, had really paid off. We had our old house, a rental house, a new house, a pickup, a car, and a tractor. Not bad, and all for $5,500. At least I didn't have to borrow forty dollars so the kids could have Christmas like I had to do one year when things were close with finances. And it only took six and a half years.

Working by the hour, I never worried much about myself, but I was pleased that I was becoming able to provide things for my family that I never had growing up during the Depression. It was tough growing up during the Depression, but we found ways to have fun. At that point in my life, I had no way to really compare my life to any other kind of life. I had thought everyone lived like my family, without anything.

In the spring of 1956. we built our first house for Sweet Lumber Company, located at Antioch and Johnson Drive, Kansas City, Kansas, for eighty cents a square foot. The only help we had was my nephew Virgil "Pee-wee" Robinson. My profit when we were finished was $180, not bad for that time. That project led to many more houses, about 2,200 or more, plus fourteen churches and about thirty Cap Homes, which was the name of a company in Minnesota.

Earl Nelson, my brother-in-law, and I worked in a partnership for nine years until he decided to go into business for himself. He thought earning all the money would be better than earning half of the money on the houses he would build on his own. As it turned out, the split worked out well for me because I was soon building about one Standard Home per week in addition to holding down a night job at Fairbanks and Morse from 11:00 a.m. until 7:00 p.m. every weekday. That began a twenty-one year stretch of working duel jobs and averaging about four hours of sleep a night.

We had to work in all kinds of weather because our houses were scheduled three to four weeks ahead. We didn't want to fall behind in the schedule for fear of losing the work and the dealership with Standard Homes. I hired four or five regular men and anyone who wanted to work part-time. I always had one good lead carpenter who got higher pay and knew more than I did about carpentry work. I had several different lead men over the years but no one to equal Pee-wee, my nephew. He worked for me until he was killed in a tragic motorcycle accident. He had never had any other regular job except the one working for me as my lead. It was hard on everyone when he was killed, and we still miss him. He had a natural instinct for carpentry. He left behind his wife, Nancy, two sons, Mitchell and Thomas, and a daughter, Vicky. I found out how the death of a very important person can change someone's life in profound ways. I never had another person as loyal as Pee Wee who worked for me. But I strove forward like a car operating on six out of eight cylinders.

We lived in our first new house for a very short time before I sold it and moved us back into the old house at 2911 until I was able to finish our second new home at 47th and Gibbs Road. That began a series of moving and building and moving and building to make a profit on my labor in the homes. It took five new houses before I moved us into a house with no payments. I have never had a payment on a house since then (or a car).

When my brother-in-law and I went our separate ways, it meant I could call my own shots and work as many hours as I wanted to keep my schedule going. When we had worked together, things just hadn't worked out. He was a good carpenter but a poor business manager. He wanted to take too much time off to enjoy the fruits of his labor, and I was more the type to work long hours to try to get ahead of schedule. "Dawn to dusk" was my motto, as I had learned as a boy and in the early stages of my marriage to Evelyn. I was living a dream of earning more money than I ever thought I would, and I did not want to lose that opportunity.

When I built my second house on 47th and Gibbs Road, I didn't know it was just over the line that separated Junction Grade School from Oak Grove Grade School. My boys wanted to finish school at Junction, so I put the house up for sale and bought a lot at 2621 S. 40th Terr. It was walking distance from the Junction school, and they were able to finish their grade school with their friends. I had moved around as a kid, eight different schools in all, and I didn't want my kids to have to go through that.

The people who bought my house at 47th and Gibbs lived in a two-and-a-half-story house on 10th and Anne, so I took it in on a trade and made it into four apartments and became a landlord. I later sold it for an $8,000 profit, plus, of course, all the rent I had collected on it while I owned it. Not bad, I would say, for an old country boy just ten or twelve years out of WWII and the Great Depression. Four great kids, a loyal wife who stood by my side through all the hard times and who became a great helpmate in running my business—not bad at all. Evelyn kept all the books and wrote all the checks to the workers for almost the entire time I ran my construction company. What more could any husband ask for? She gave her all.

I built a house on 40th Street and Shawnee Drive, one block away from the 40th Terr. property, and we moved there when the boys were in seventh and eighth grades. They were old enough too be good help on construction jobs, but they were young and would rather play baseball and basketball with their neighborhood chums and against each other. They did not have the same ambition that I had at their age. They were more interested in playing than working. I had always thought play was a waste of time and energy, so it was hard for me to watch and allow them to "waste" time playing when I knew how hard I'd had it as a young man. So there was much conflict between my boys and me over what I viewed as the "modern way" of play before work and the way I had learned, which was work before play—and almost no play at that. Both my sons grew up to be successful in business and teaching, so I guess I must have taught them something right with my "old ways" of thinking.

Joyce had a tough time, being the oldest, because she was assigned most of the work helping her mother around the house. She also did a lot of babysitting for her brothers. Audrey helped around the house, too, with dishes and other housework. The girls were already almost grown and were into the business of boyfriends. On the issue of boyfriends, both the girls were very pretty and did not have a shortage of male suitors when they were teenagers.

Chapter 20

Finally, Johnson County

OUR FIRST FARM, **on Highway 69 in Stillwell, Kansas, 1961, forty-three years old**

We lived in the Junction School District until the girls were out of high school and the boys were in seventh and eight grades. At that milestone, I thought I could start looking for the farm I had longed for since I came home from the merchant marines and WWII.

I had built many houses south on Highway 69, so one day when I drove by a farm that had a for-sale sign up, I stopped to inquire about the price. They were asking $45,000 for it, but I thought that was a little too much money, so I didn't give it much thought until a month later. We'd had about a three- or four-week span of really wet weather, and as I was coming home from work, I saw that the for-sale sign was still there. The owner had moved to the Lake of the Ozarks, so I stopped to look again. The basement was full of water because, as we found later, the drain had been plugged during that wet spell.

I drove from there and stopped at the real estate company's office. The realtor wanted me to give an offer on the land, and I offered $25,000. He said he would call the owner and let me know. To my surprise, when I arrived home he had already called. I called him back and found out that, lo and behold, the owners had accepted my offer, $20,000 below their asking price.

I closed the deal the following day, before they could get a better offer and back out. The place had not been lived in for part of that year, so it needed a good cleaning and some repairs. Building business was slow in the winter of 1961, so I had time to work on it. My sons both helped on weekends, and I used one regular man and some part-time help to do the work. We redid all the walls, ceilings, and floors and put in new kitchen cabinets and a new furnace. I put on a new roof, installed a new septic system, and built a new detached garage. When we moved in, it was like moving into a brand-new home.

We moved in early spring, so David and Stephen had a few weeks of school left. They were too young to drive, so they stayed with their sister Joyce and her new husband, Kenny Ogle, to finish out the school year. I moved to the farm with Evelyn and was very proud to live there. I was liking my life pretty well. I bought two horses for the boys, one, a palomino that David helped train. He learned to be a really good horseman. He rode bareback every time he got on the horse.

I also bought some calves that the boys helped raise and bottle feed as well as other random cattle at sales and from here and there. I thought I was doing just fine until the boys started attending Stillwell High School. They did not feel they were getting the same quality of education they had received at Turner High School and both felt like fish out of water. I made the hard decision to give up my lifelong dream and sell the farm so we could move back into town for the benefit of all concerned.

I had built my brother Donald a house on that farm, so I made a trade with my other brother, Virgil, for his house, which was located where everyone could get back to business as usual before we moved to the farm. The boys were very glad to be reunited with the friends they had spent so many years growing up with on 42nd Street. (Virgil's house was on 42nd St., too.) I sold the house my brother traded me because we didn't like the house or the location very well. It had a very small yard for the boys. I bought a little two-bedroom home in Highland Crest that we lived in until I could build a better house with more of a yard at 47th and Berry, just up 47th Street from our previous Gibbs Road house, that was on the corner of Gibbs and 47th. We liked that house and location so much that we thought we would not move again until the boys were through with high school and I could buy another farm.

Plans changed. We had lived in this location for about a year when someone wanted to buy the house because he liked the location. He made me an offer and I refused it. About a week later, he came back with an offer for $2,000 more. Again, I told him that the house was not for sale. I told my wife that if he made me one more offer, I would probably accept. Sure enough, he came back a week later and offered more money. I told him he could have the house when I found a lot to build our next house on.

I found a lot on the corner of Gibbs Road and 47th Street at a diagonal location from our first house on 47th Street. So that was three houses I built and lived in on the same street. I had gotten about $6,000 dollars above the market price for the other house because the man wanted it so much. It had been a nice three-bedroom ranch house with a nice place for a garden and a roomy lot. Not a bad deal for me, though we didn't like giving up the location.

During our time in the house on 47th and Gibbs Road was a really busy time in my building career. While framing that house, we were also framing one house or more a week for

Standard Homes. I had also built a church at 22nd and Steel Road. We attended that church for the next twelve years until the pastor ended up falling to some temptations of the flesh and we left to escape the scandal.

I built a house for a black Baptist preacher at 38th and Metropolitan Road in Argentine, Kansas, part of Kansas City. I later built a church for him in the same neighborhood. He was a nice man to work with and later recommended me to a black Methodist group at 10th and Anne, who I helped build a church.

I saw that I was through building churches because it was a venture that reaped very little profit, except maybe in the heavenly kingdom. I never felt right charging the going prices for my services and was lucky to break even on those projects. As it turns out, there were still several more churches in my future, whether I wanted to build them or not. The next one was built on County Line Road in Johnson County. It was a Church of Christ congregation. It was about then that I moved to the farm in Johnson County.

My second farm was located in Spring Hill, Kansas, Johnson County, 19475 West 167th St. I was forty-four when I bought it. When Joyce married her second husband, Bob Lillich, I got him a job with my basement contractor, running a high-loader and digging basements. As he traveled down Highway 169 one day on the way home from one of his jobs, he saw a for-sale sign for an 80-acre farm. The farm was to be sold on the courthouse steps in Olathe, Kansas, the following week. I took Evelyn to the auction on a bleak, rainy day and outbid everyone else for $28,000. It was located next to some railroad tracks and had great rich soil to plant or raise cattle on.

I built a house on the property for Bob and Joyce to live in so they could watch over the property while I remained in Kansas City to allow my two sons to finish high school over the next two years. Joyce and Bob, however, decided they did not like country living and ended up moving into town after about a year. At that point, Stephen still had part of his senior year to finish at Turner High School and David was going to Kansas City Junior College. I didn't want the house to stand vacant on the farm, so we moved to the farm and my sons drove back and forth to school in the 1956 Chevy that they both shared. That car serviced a lot of people before it bit the dust, including my nephew Pee-wee and another nephew of Bob's and was still running well when I ended up selling it to someone else.

Moving to the farm meant I would need a building for livestock and a machine shop for my construction business. I built a thirty-by-forty-foot sheep barn and a twenty-four-by-sixty-foot machine shop with a sixty-by-forty-foot shed off to the side. A well company dug us a 190-foot-deep well for water.

At about the same time, Sweet Lumber Company moved their company one mile from my farm, at the intersection of I-35 and 169 Highway, which made things really convenient for me and my building business. But I still had to make a twenty-mile drive back and forth during the week to my night job at Fairbanks and Morse in Kansas City. I made that drive for the next thirteen years where I worked the night shift and worked days building houses.

A lot of my jobs building houses were located north of where my night job was located, so my crew would meet me on the job, so I didn't need to go home. David, Stephen, and Evelyn did what needed to be done on the farm, such as feeding the calves and lambs, mowing, taking care of the garden, cleaning the barns, etc. I did the rest when I got home from the construction job. Then I would eat supper and catch a few winks before I went off to my night job at Fairbanks. I caused my wife some worry over whether I would fall asleep at the wheel on the way to work, but that was the way life was, and that was the way it would be for the next thirteen years, working at two jobs and keeping a farm running. I guess it proves that hard work doesn't kill you and that the old adage is true: "What doesn't kill us, makes us stronger."

Because I was raised on a farm and worked for some big farmers in Minnesota, long hours and hard physical labor was nothing new for me, but the boys were doing things they had never done before. They seemed to learn fast, but they were not exactly the most enthusiastic farm workers I could have had helping me. They did a lot of complaining. I guess they just didn't understand the nature of farm work. They were strong enough physically, but mentally they didn't exactly buy into the whole process. Maybe if I had owned a farm when they were young boys they would have grown better accustomed to the work and maybe even liked it.

As it was, they never wanted to farm, and as I grew older, the farm eventually became too much for me to manage while they were off building their careers in other occupations. As I mentioned earlier, they are both successful and not afraid of hard work in the professions they chose. I guess if nothing else I at least taught them the value of perseverance and that hard work equals life.

That concludes my recollections up to this point in my life. At my ripe old age of 100 I am still delivering papers to the doorsteps of the "old people' in the neighborhood. Hello up there, Evelyn. I'll be up there in the twinkling of an eye, as the old church song says, soon as I pound this one last nail.

Epilogue

Notes from Sons, David and Stephen

WHILE OUR FATHER'S writing ends here, we both decided to add a biographical summary that we used at his one hundredth birthday celebration last year, which will perhaps add a few more insights and a greater sense of closure to a life lived well, healthily, and with dedication to his family, his church, his cattle, his farm, and his home-building career.

Balancing those loyalties was never an easy task, as one might imagine, especially when he existed on about four hours of sleep a night and catnaps for most of his working life. Holding down two jobs and running a cattle business required never-ending adjustments to family demands. He worked in construction into his early eighties.

In this book, our father has provided some stories about that individual struggle and of his victories over hardship. At the time of this writing, he is still kicking and waiting for his 101st birthday on December 18, 2018. The summary that follows will hopefully give the reader a wider sense of his accomplishments in more encapsulated form and perhaps include some information he has not already covered. He wanted to include this in the book even though his own writing would have been more than suffiecient to tell his story.

Biography of Emery Carl Hinkhouse Jr., written by Stephen E. Hinkhouse

WHEN A MAN has lived one hundred years, it is nearly impossible to write a short summary of his life. However, by viewing his childhood, early adulthood and family, work accomplishments, and church affiliations, it is possible to illuminate important events that defined his existence. It may be difficult for generations that followed Emery to recognize the myriad trails he has traveled. Let's start with his childhood and paint a picture of how this difficult period in his life molded his mores, habits, and opinions for the rest of his days.

Emery was born in Correctionville, Iowa, on December 18, 1917 and became a member of what would later be called America's Greatest Generation. Unknown to him for several decades, one month before his birth, on November 7, Vladimir Lenin had led the Bolsheviks in the second Russian Revolution to depose Tsar Nicholas II and begin the communist experiment he believed would change the world.

A few months after Emery was born, World War I, the Great War, had just ended. Three years after his birth, the Nineteenth Amendment was added to the US Constitution, which allowed women to vote. In Emery's first decade, the car, airplane, telephone, indoor plumbing, gas stove, and even electricity were unavailable for most rural families like his own. Emery was living American history, not just reading about it.

Emery Carl Hinkhouse, Jr.

Anyone who has seen the movie or read the book *Grapes of Wrath* by John Steinbeck can visualize the childhood and early adulthood that Emery lived. In fact, he rode huddled under a blanket in the back of an open-air Model T touring car on a snowy, cold winter day as his mother and new stepfather drove from his birth home in Iowa to Oklahoma to start a new life. As hard as he tried, he was unable to see his future clearly, as the Great Depression had already begun in Oklahoma and Missouri and many lives were being blighted by lack of opportunity.

Emery's life became one of survival during the late 1920s and most of the 1930s. Not only the loss of jobs but also an elongated, multiyear drought defined the Depression in the center of America. His experiences were not dissimilar, and in fact may have been worse in many ways, to any movie or snapshot anyone has seen depicting this terrible time in America.

His family moved to seemingly uncountable places, tenant farms, in Oklahoma, Missouri, Kansas, and Nebraska in the 1920s, looking for opportunities to work for his father and even Emery as a young boy and teenager. He learned about farming, dairy operations, making corn liquor—which his stepfather sold illegally—and hunting. Each of these life skills were primary to Emery, as schooling became a secondary goal because of financial stresses on his family. Because of his constant uprooting and schooling changes, it was hard for him to follow a learning schedule with consistent continuity and even harder to make and keep friends, as his stays in some locations lasted not much longer than a year. Playground confrontations and after-school fighting seemed necessary to Emery in order to position himself on the alpha male ladder each time he moved to a new school. After many of these moves, he found some constancy living in Vernon County, Missouri, most notably in Montevallo and later in Nevada.

Little did he know that prohibition of alcohol, a stock market crash, and a national bank failure would occur in his childhood and teenage years. In 1933, during his junior year in high school, he joined three hundred thousand other young men in the Civilian Conservation Corps program, established by his hero, President Franklin Delano Roosevelt, to provide his family with a secondary financial resource for existence. To earn thirty dollars each month, he drove trucks, shoveled dirt, lifted boulders, and learned the value of hard physical labor as he and his companions in the CCC built damns, planted trees, and molded landscapes to beautify and improve transportation access across America.

The program required that he send a minimum of twenty-five dollars home to his parents for the support of his brothers, Virgil and Donald, and his sister, Goldie. To make extra money, he used his fighting skills and became a boxer in weekend exhibitions across Missouri. He met Carl Arnold in the CCCs, and he became a lifelong friend.

After two stints in the CCC, early adulthood arrived for Emery and he left home again to find work back in Iowa. He did what he knew best and hired himself out to farmers as a field worker or dairy labor. Shelling corn, milking cows, and baling hay were jobs he knew how to do. But he knew this kind of labor would not offer him an opportunity to improve his station in life. So he tried new ideas: hauling flax, the PWA (Public Works Administration), hanging electric wires for Co-Op Electric, and finally, the National Guard. He finagled his way into the PWA job opportunity by getting an exception to work, as only heads of household were allowed to have these jobs. This was one of many times in his life that Emery found a way to get around the rules and regulations that restricted most other people from his generation.

Later, the last years of the 1930s seemed like lost years to Emery. He had been back and forth between his Nevada home and working in Iowa. In 1940, while visiting the Lincoln Hotel in St. James, Minnesota, where he got a job tending bar, he decided to take a change of pace from the bar scene and walked down the street to the Sweet Shop. When he walked in, he soon saw his friend Merle Miller with his girlfriend, Ellen. Alongside them was Evelyn Nelson, eighteen years old and more beautiful than anyone he had ever seen. Emery learned Evelyn would be at Lake Okoboji the next night, and he found her there with her brother, Harold. He was polite and asked Harold if he could court her. He and Evelyn both knew immediately that they would spend their lives together, and in January 1941 they married in St. James. The rest of the 1940s would not be less difficult for him and his new wife; World War II was on the horizon, and a wave of national pride swept across America.

After his first two children were born, Joyce in St. James and Audrey in Nevada, and farming had not offered the financial success Emery craved, he moved his family to Kansas City, Kansas. The country became embroiled in WWII in both the Pacific and Europe. Any male and many females felt it their duty to serve and fight. After failed attempts to enlist in the army and navy because of eyesight issues, Emery finally tricked the examiner conducting the merchant marine physical exams and enlisted for service in the Pacific. He trained in Sheepshead Bay in Brooklyn, New York, and noticed that his time spent in the CCC and the National Guard made his assimilation into the merchant marines easier than it was for many of his eventual shipmates. Only time would tell if his marriage could survive the dislocation that war would cause his family.

Emery chose to serve in war zones because the pay was better. He didn't really understand the peril he would endure as his ship, the Joseph A. Kinyoun, delivered and picked up goods in Okinawa, Saipan, and the Philippines. In retrospect, the fact that his ship survived the historic Okinawa typhoon seems nothing less than a miracle, as 80 percent of the ships in that storm perished at sea or were marooned at Buckner Bay or Yellow Beach.

Emery returned from the war thirteen months after most soldiers, as his ship's duties included war-zone "cleanup" and transporting goods back to America. He arrived back home to greet his wife and girls, not only having survived the war but somehow having avoided malaria and a foot disease called jungle rot. His family was now intact, and it was time to begin a new life.

He and our family ended up settling down in Kansas City, Kansas, where he and Evelyn produced two young boys, David and Stephen. They would eventually move from the middle of town to what was then the suburbs of Kansas City, in the Maple Hill area on 42nd Street. We attended Junction Grade School and Turner High School with fellow members of the bulging generation of postwar babies, later to be named the baby boomers, children whose value system became radically different than their parents'.

Emery found work as an electrician and later as a boiler tender at Fairbanks & Morse, and he encouraged both his brothers to work there, too. Virgil became a skilled machinist, and Donald eventually became coowner of the plant. Emery has deep pride for having seen both of his brothers flourish in their careers at Fairbanks. But working as an hourly employee wasn't enough for him.

In the mid 1950s, with Evelyn's brother Earl, Emery began a new career, building houses. Together, and later separately, they participated in the building boom of housing for growing families with baby boomer children. They offered rough-in services for standard homes, pre-cut "vanilla" house choices for middle-class suburbanites. Emery kept his night job at Fairbanks and joined the crew with Earl during the day. There were weeks he worked more than eighty hours at both jobs to keep the money flowing into the household. Sleep and family affairs had to take back seat to his appetite for work and wealth accumulation during this phase of his life.

His financial success was enormous, relatively speaking, and he was able to purchase farm grounds in Olathe, Kansas, and send his sons to college—an activity no Hinkhouse had previously attempted because, even in that day, college was considered an expensive enterprise that many parents could not afford to provide for their children. We remember he had what he called his "college-educated cow," whose milk he raised calves on; he spent the money he made from those calves to help us go to college at Kansas University (KU). He concocted innumerable ways of providing extra income for his family during those inflationary times.

Joyce, Audrey, David, and Stephen all married and had a total of twelve children, followed by twenty-three grandchildren. Joyce married Bob Lillich, and together they had three children and subsequently nine grandchildren and now five great-grandchildren. Audrey married, had two children with her first husband, and later married Alan Haskins. Together, they had a third child and they now have four grandchildren. David and Stephen attended KU and graduated. Dad was proud of this, as no other Hinkhouse had accomplished that. David worked with Emery for a while after college and then decided to pursue a teaching career with his wife, Kathy, in New York. Together, they had three children and three grandchildren. He and his wife, Donna, had three children and seven grandchildren. Emery can relish his legacy as he sits and pontificates with his neighborhood friends about the different paths all of his offspring have traveled behind him in their lives.

It is important to recognize the contributions Emery made to his churches during his life. He and his wife, Evelyn, together found their Lord in the early 1950s as they attended a service led by Reverend Chance and later Nellie Brooks and Brother Lyles. Emery helped to pioneer four different churches, all Assembly of God. First was Maple Hill Assembly on 42nd Street. He actually helped build the building for this church. It was an experience he duplicated three more times: Gospel Temple, Liberty Assembly, and Abundant Life. Emery not only helped build the physical structures at each of these churches, but he also offered weekly attendance, tithing, and additional financial support when called upon. If God had one main calling for Emery, it was as a church builder.

Emery lived through the Great Depression, served in WWII, learned many skills, worked many jobs, flourished as a house builder, raised a family, watched human rights improve, and served his Lord. His accomplishments stand behind no one, considering his meager beginnings, limited opportunities, and the challenging obstacles he encountered. His work ethic defines him. His family and friends remain to tell the story of his life to their own children and grandchildren and the many generations to follow, a story of hard work, perseverance, and an unselfish commitment to family and friends.

Emery Carl Hinkhouse, Jr.

The following poems and the one in the introduction were written by my son, David with his permission.

Bottom of the Well

All night long she mooed and at dawn when we
found her at the well's bottom--
the dried up well that we no longer used--
she still had some fight in her though her voice,
the voice I heard all night through the window screen,
the desperate moan of a moo moo-moan that drowned out
every other sound, the sound of fear and pain in ugly mix,
the moo-moan that comes back to haunt my dreams,
sounded resigned to fate. With one leg awry,
pointed at the red morning sky,
and a pitiful moo-moan, she cast me a wild-eyed stare
right before I put her out of misery with my Smith Wesson.
I scooped dirt on top of her to block out memory
but it comes back to haunt. I make promises
of never again. I cover my tracks
so no one falls into the craters
I create. I listen for the moo-moan
and keep the rescue equipment handy
because I cannot forget the voice
of desperation, the moo-moan.

Out Past the Paved Path: Dust Bowl Stories My Father Told Me

The road turned to gravel before our place.
On the paved road, women hired maids to dust.
Around our home, dust defined the landscape.
It created a foggy haze all day long. Even
the marigolds grew sickly and lost the luster
they were supposed to provide, no matter how
often we watered and rinsed them. Mom
pulled out the Pine-Sol, a bucket of soapy water
and an old rag almost every day, but we
still had to wipe dust off the plates and glasses
before we ate or drank. It formed black rings
around my brother's and my shirtless waists
in July and August. We yearned for the smell
of rain and hated the morning sun. As the heat
dragged across the days, the hard frown deepened
in my father's face. We spent our days squatting
in shade under the cottonwoods. We swatted at flies--
watched the garden vegetables and the bed of petunias
shrivel and hang limp like the worry wrinkles
in Mother's face turned, by degree, downward
into a fixed scowl. The hens quit laying eggs
in the shed. We breathed dust, ate dust, and spit it
back out. The sun used the dust for paint,
and we were its canvas. The dry wind used dust
to write couplets through the barns eaves and we
were its stanza. Dust rose like wind-driven snow,
up against the house and through the curtains. The sun
sapped hope—the soybeans planted in spring
before the drought, the brougham grass pastures the cattle

Emery Carl Hinkhouse, Jr.

chewed down to stubble, the cattle dying one by one,
the dried-up well by the house. The grasshoppers seemed
to thrive on our thirst--the dust itself. We had to wait it out.
We narrowed our list of prayers to wailing cries for rain.
We memorized the lessons of dust taught in the school
of empty haylofts and the litany of our parents' prayers.

Ya gotta be smarter than the cow,

my dad used to yell at me when we
rounded up cattle for vaccinations,
castration, and dehorning. We did not
own a horse, so my brother, our cur dog
and our mongrel father made an ever-tightening
half circle around the herd of mixed-breed cows
of every color and mottled markings. We would
wave our arms like a philharmonic conductor
to indicate direction while the fearless mutt
nipped at their heels and headed them,
yapping, to the corral and the vet's torture chamber—
a vaccination chute that closed around their necks
and kept them from escaping the pain
we were about to inflict. In every herd
there was one mean bull who had different ideas
about travel plans than we did. He seemed to know
what awaited him in the chute. He would break
loose from the circle and charge right toward me--
me waving my hands back and forth like a heavy bird
trying to take flight off a lake, then dodging
to the side avoiding attack like a matador
(minus red cape) as he made his way back
to the freedom of the green grass--temporarily.
We would widen the circle again and point the mutt
in the direction of the wayward bull, no lesson
learned on my part about how to be smarter than a cow,
and definitely not as smart as a dog.

Made in United States
Troutdale, OR
07/15/2023